BE A MENSCH!

Be a MENSCH

Why Good Character Is the Key to a Life of
Happiness, Health, Wealth, and Love

AN ANTHOLOGY COMPILED BY
MOSHE KAPLAN, MD

gefen
publishing house בית הוצאה לאור גפן
JERUSALEM ♦ NEW YORK

Grateful permission is acknowledged to the following for reproduction of excerpts in chapter 7:

"A Moment of Victory," reproduced from *The Gift of Speech: Refining the Way We Speak* by Rabbi Shimon Finkelstein, with permission of the copyright holders, ArtScroll/Mesorah Publications, Ltd.

"Of Angels and Poinsettias," reproduced by permission of Aish.com and Sara Yoheved Rigler.

"The Blue Skirt," reproduced from *A Sunny Slice of Life: Looking Up When Life Tries to Pull You Down* by Malka Adler, with permission of the copyright holders, Targum Press.

"The Tzaddik Who Ruled through His Fear of Heaven: Sixty-one Years since the Martyrdom of HaRav Avrohom Grodzensky, *zt"l, Hy"d*," by M. Musman, with permission of the copyright holders, © 2005 *Yated Ne'eman*, Bnei Brak, Israel.

Design & Typesetting: KPS, Jerusalem
Cover Design: S. Kim Glassman
ISBN 978-965-229-433-3

1   3   5   7   9   8   6   4   2

Gefen Publishing House, Ltd.   Gefen Books
6 Hatzvi Street, Jerusalem 94386, Israel   600 Broadway, Lynbrook, NY 11563, USA
972-2-538-0247   516-593-1234
orders@gefenpublishing.com   orders@gefenpublishing.com

www.israelbooks.com

Printed in Israel   *Send for our free catalogue*

הרב לוי יצחק הלוי הורוויץ

בן אאמו"ר הרה"צ פד"ה זצוק"ל מבוסטון

Grand Rabbi Levi I. Horowitz

"*To Be a Mensch* addresses a central problem of our times: what is good character, and why should we care about it? We can all see the decline in honest concern for others, idealism, responsibility for the community, and the drive to have a life that makes the world a better place. Historically, religion has been the source of these values. Dr. Moshe Kaplan is continuing this tradition in the present volume by gathering together an all-star group of people with advanced secular education and profound religious commitment. Their articles explore good character from many perspectives: psychological, economic, philosophical, physical and more. This will provide food for thought and inspiration for those seeking a more meaningful approach to life. I wish Dr. Kaplan and his authors every success in inspiring people to raise their sights and seek more idealistic and meaningful lives."

Bostoner Rebbe

מעלות האדמו"ר מבוסטון 1 ת.ד. 43033 הר נוף, ירושלים 02-651-9688 1 *Maalot Hadmor MiBoston, P.O.B. 43033 Har Nof, Jerusalem, Israel 02-651-9688*

This book is dedicated to the memory of

HaGaon HaRav Chaim Kreisworth, *zt"l.*

Praised and loved by all who knew him, his brilliance, warmth and deliberate, polite and modest good character inspired a generation. It was a gift to be close to such a saintly soul.

Acknowledgment

Some of the ideas recorded in this book were presented to me by my own teachers and others and are not essentially mine. To them I am indebted, especially to Rabbi Beryl Gershenfeld, who is the embodiment of a mensch. Others who helped with this book are Jake Greenberg, who provided valuable editorial and composition assistance, and the professional, reliable, and knowledgeable staff of Gefen Publishing House, who provided insightful review and instructive comments.

I am of course profoundly grateful to the contributing authors, especially Rabbi Dovid Gottlieb with his invaluable ideas. And certainly I want to express my appreciation to G-d for the inspiration and to my wife, Karen, for her support in making this book a reality.

Contents

Author Biographies

Sara Yoheved Rigler is a graduate of Brandeis University. Her spiritual journey took her to India and through fifteen years of teaching Vedanta philosophy and meditation. Since 1985, she has been practicing Torah Judaism. Her articles have appeared in *Jewish Women Speak about Jewish Matters, Chicken Soup for the Jewish Soul*, and Heaven on Earth. She is the author of the bestseller *Holy Woman* and the new *Lights from Jerusalem*. She is also a featured writer on Aish.com, the world's largest Judaism website. She lives in the Old City of Jerusalem with her husband and children.

Rabbi Abraham J. Twerski, MD, is the founder and medical director emeritus of Gateway Rehabilitation Center, a nationally recognized not-for-profit drug and alcohol treatment system in western Pennsylvania. An ordained rabbi, Dr. Twerski held a pulpit until 1959 when he graduated from Marquette University Medical School and went on to complete his psychiatric residency at the University of Pittsburgh Western Psychiatric Institute. For twenty years, he served as clinical director of the Department of Psychiatry at St. Francis Hospital, Pittsburgh, and currently is an associate professor of psychiatry at the University of Pittsburgh School of Medicine. A frequent lecturer on a broad range of topics, including stress, self-esteem, and spirituality, as well as chemical dependency, Dr. Twerski has also written over sixty books and articles.

Howard Jonas is the founder and CEO of International Discount Telecommunications (IDT), a billion-dollar alternate communications carrier. Born in the Bronx, New York, he graduated from Bronx High School of Science and Harvard University. He lives in the Bronx with his wife and eight children.

Professor Robert J. Aumann, PhD was born in Frankfurt-am-Main, Germany, and emigrated as a child to New York. He received his bachelor's degree from City College of New York, and a PhD in mathematics from MIT. He has taught in the mathematics department of the Hebrew University of Jerusalem since 1956. In 1990, he was among the founders of the Center for Rationality at the Hebrew University, an interdisciplinary research center for Game Theory. Aumann is the author of well over eighty research papers and six books, and has held visiting positions at Princeton, Yale, Berkeley, Louvain, Stanford, Stony Brook, and NYU. In 2005 he was awarded the Alfred Nobel Memorial Prize in Economic Sciences for his work in Game Theory.

Yakir Kaufman was born in Haifa and received his MD from the Hebrew University Hadassah Faculty of Medicine in 1994. In 1995 he became a resident doctor at the Department of Neurology of the Hadassah University Hospital in Jerusalem. Dr. Kaufman is a member of the Israeli Neurological Society and junior member of the American Academy of Neurology. With his wife and children, he is currently in Toronto, Canada, where he has been appointed a fellow in the Behavioral Neurology Program at the Baycrest Centre for Geriatric Care and the Rotman Institute. His areas of research include Psychoneuroimmunology and the link between spirituality and health.

Malcolm Hoenlein is the executive vice chairman of the Conference of Presidents of Major American Jewish Organizations since June 1986. He was the founding executive director of the Greater New York Conference on Soviet Jewry and the Jewish Community Relations Council of New York. Born in Philadelphia, Pennsylvania, Hoenlein received his BA from Temple University and his PhD from the University of Pennsylvania. He has taught international relations and served as a Middle East specialist at the Foreign Policy Research Institute (FPRI). In addition, he served on the editorial staff of *Orbis*, FPRI's journal of international affairs. Hoenlein is the recipient of many awards and tributes. He serves on the Board of Directors or Advisory Board of several companies, including Bank Leumi USA. He is also the Director of Keryx Biopharmaceuticals since 2001.

Rabbi Dovid Gottlieb received his PhD in mathematical logic from Brandeis University before teaching philosophy at Johns Hopkins University. He received a National Science Foundation Research Grant, and published the resulting findings in *Ontological Economy* (Oxford University Press, 1980). In 1990 he published *The Informed Soul: An Introduction to Jewish Philosophy* with Mesorah. In 1981 he moved to Jerusalem with his family to teach at Ohr Somayach Rabbinical College.

Judith Mishell, PhD, is a clinical psychologist, author, and educator. She received her MS and PhD in psychology from Rutgers University. She has held faculty posts at Douglass College,

Rutgers University and Medical School, the California School of Professional Psychology, and the Department of Pediatrics of the UCLA Medical School. She taught at Bais Yaakov Los Angeles and the Women's Torah Institute of Yeshiva of Los Angeles. Dr. Mishell is the coauthor with Rabbi Shalom Srebrenik, PhD, of *Beyond Your Ego: A Torah Approach to Psychological Health, Inner Harmony, and Self-Knowledge* (CIS Publishers, 1991) and author of numerous essays including "When Someone's Life Is in Your Hands," in *Shidduchim, Shalom Bayis, and Beyond: Building a Bayis Ne'eman B'Yisroel* (Mesorah, 2005). She is now in private practice in Jerusalem and is a professor of psychology at the Moreshet Institute at Neve Yerushalayim.

Moshe Kaplan, MD, is a trained psycho-immunologist, using mind, body, and soul integration for optimal health and healing. In college, he was an All-American lacrosse player. While serving as a major in the United States Armed Forces he received the Igor Sikorsky helicopter Rescue Award for valor in saving seamen's lives. He was a cofounder of Wellness Medical Clinics applying wellness concepts to practical reality. In conjunction with Naomi Remen, MD, at Stanford Medical School, he received a grant from the National Institute of Mental Health to write a curriculum for medical schools to use as a model for an ideal health care delivery system integrating professionals, paraprofessionals, and laypeople. He is the compiler of *A Wholly Life* (Targum Press, 2005). Currently, besides being an author and an investment advisor, he is a medical director of Magen David Adom in Jerusalem, where he lives with his wife Karen.

Introduction

Sara Yoheved Rigler, *author of* Holy Woman *and* Lights from Jerusalem

In high school, I was chosen by my class as "Most Likely to Succeed." For the yearbook picture, the photographer threw a pile of $1 bills on the floor, bid me to sit nearby, and made me pose reaching for the money. This was the photographer's concept of "success."

Ironically, in the four decades since that photo was snapped, I have probably made less money than anyone else in my class. However, as far as I'm concerned, my life has been tremendously successful. You see, I never considered my goal to be amassing money, but rather to grow spiritually.

Of course you want to succeed in life, but "success" depends on what your goal is. If you are playing hockey, you had better know which goal is your team's. Otherwise, you could (as I once did, to my tremendous embarrassment) hit your puck into the wrong goal and end up scoring for the other team.

According to Judaism, the goal of life is to fix one's character xviii · *Be a Mensch!*

traits: if one is stingy, to become more generous; if one is anger-prone, to become more patient; if one routinely lies or cheats, to become more honest. In other words, the goal of life according to Judaism is to become a mensch.

Unfortunately, a survey of young people's life goals today is less likely to name "character development" than:

- Wealth
- Fame
- Romance
- Professional achievement
- Academic accomplishments
- Artistic success

The greatness of this book is that its editor, Dr. Moshe Kaplan, has assembled people who have achieved the above goals, and they are telling us that the most important achievement in life is character development.

For example, Howard Jonas is the founder and CEO of a multibillion-dollar company, and he writes: "Good character, which is at least as essential [as talent and luck], if not more so, to founding and running a major company, can be developed." Professor Robert Aumann won the Nobel Prize in economics, the pinnacle of academic achievement, and he writes: "Game Theory recognizes those modes of behavior that we call 'good character traits' as ways to foster cooperation in repeated interactions and to provide a person with an enhanced social existence." In layman's terms that means: Good character builds stable, positive relationships.

Most people in the twenty-first century consider character development as old-fashioned as cassette tapes and videos; they're worth nothing on eBay. Even a cursory glance at corporate America or Capitol Hill shows that virtues such as honesty or fidelity are considered less worth striving for than a good golf score.

Even those who appreciate the virtue of virtue relegate it to secondary importance – not a vocation, but an avocation; not a career, but a hobby. And who today has time for hobbies? Most men have no more time to develop empathy than they do to put together a model airplane. Most women are as little interested in overcoming anger as in crocheting and needlepoint. Yet character development requires time, energy, and commitment. Why bother?

The authors of *Be a Mensch!* tell us why to bother. Howard Jonas assures us that good character is good business. Malcolm Hoenlein, one of the major Jewish leaders in America, confides that the secret of successful leadership is developing positive character traits that enhance our ability to work with others. Dr. Yakir Kaufman proves, citing scientific studies, that good character traits are the key to good health. Rabbi Dr. Dovid Gottlieb demonstrates why character development is essential to tapping our maximum potential. Psychologist Dr. Judith Mishell explores the extensive psychological benefits of good character, such as greater happiness and self-esteem.

The happiness factor is key here. People formulate their life goals according to what they believe will bring them happiness and fulfillment. All of the goals mentioned in the bulleted list above, such as wealth, fame, romance, and professional achievement, are really just means to the ultimate goal of happiness. People don't want wealth so they can run their hands through piles of money (the yearbook photographer notwithstanding). People want wealth in order to acquire the possessions and lifestyle they believe will make them happy.

If you could be convinced that you are more likely to

be happy by working on the trait of kindness than by working twelve-hour days on Wall Street, wouldn't you shift your priorities?

Deep down, we all admire sterling character traits more than wealth, fame, or reaching the top of the corporate ladder. We might want to be as rich as Bill Gates or as famous as Julia Roberts, but our *admiration* is elicited more by the fellow who, last year, jumped down onto the tracks of the New York City subway system in front of an oncoming train in order to save the life of someone who had fallen there. His courage and altruism inspired a flood of media praise, public recognition, and medals, because we all know true greatness when we see it.

After Princess Di was killed, all of the articles eulogizing her emphasized not her wealth and glamour, but her kindness and empathy, how she visited homeless shelters and took the time to speak with the impoverished people there. You will never attend a memorial service and hear, "We will miss Gloria. She was so well dressed." You are more likely to hear, "We will miss Gloria. She was so generous." And what counts at the end is what counts all along.

This book will change your life if you let it. Of course, you can no more acquire good character traits by reading this book than you can acquire a great wardrobe by poring over the Lands' End catalogue. *Be A Mensch!*, like a good catalogue, lets you know what's available to be had and gives you the impetus to want to acquire it. Then you have to *do something*, such as practicing techniques that build character and finding role models to emulate.

The success of developing your character, unlike the success of wealth or fame, is entirely in your own hands. After much hard work, you may become the best actor in Hollywood, but without a "big break," you'll still be waiting tables. If, on the other hand, you work hard on developing integrity, you will acquire it. More than that, you will become it. You are not just "likely to succeed." You are guaranteed to succeed.

Chapter 1

A Truly Holistic Approach

Rabbi Abraham J. Twerski, MD, *Founder and Medical Director Emeritus of the Gateway Rehabilitation Center, and the author of over thirty books on personal growth*

The pursuit of happiness is universal, but there is no unanimity as to what constitutes happiness. The advances of science, technology, and medicine have resulted in the availability of previously undreamt-of sources of comfort and pleasure. Among my patients were some of the world's wealthiest people, who had the means to get anything and everything they desired, yet they were in my office, because of either depression or drug addiction. Saturated with pleasure but frustrated that they were not getting anywhere, they were living proof of Philip Brickman's observation that Western civilization is on a "hedonistic treadmill."

In the account of creation in Genesis, God created everything, from the tiniest insect to the leviathan, from a grain of sand to supergalaxies. However, when He was about to create a human being, we find a strange expression: "And God said, 'Let *us* make man.'" *Us*? Whose help was God enlisting, and why did

He create everything in the universe without anyone's participation, yet apparently could not create man by Himself?

The Baal Shem Tov explained that everything in the universe was created in a state of completion. Little bears grow to be big bears, but do not change themselves. The transformation of a caterpillar to a butterfly is not a volitional act by the caterpillar, but rather a metamorphosis programmed into its genes. Angels, too, were created complete. God, for reasons known only to Him, wanted to have a being that would be different from any other creature, in that it would be created incomplete, in a state of potential, and by its own effort would strive towards perfection. This creature would be "man." God could have created man in a state of completion, but then man would have been either an animal or an angel, not the being that God wished.

Therefore, the Baal Shem Tov said, God says to man, "Let *us* make man," you and I together. I will give you the potential to become man, but you must develop that potential, and by your own effort, become the "man" that I desire.

A human being enters this world in essentially an animal state, "pure *id*," as Freud would say, seeking only the gratification of his desires. If a person remains totally driven by his desires, seeking to fulfill the "pleasure principle" and restrained only by the desire to avoid pain, "the reality principle," then he has not advanced beyond the animal stage. Yes, he may be intelligent, but is only an intelligent animal, or as science designates him, *homo sapiens* – an intellectual baboon.

Homo sapiens can achieve contentment, but as Carnation milk's slogan, "Milk from contented cows," indicates, contentment is an appropriate measure of excellence for a cow, but not for a human being.

Hedonistic man (an oxymoron) cannot be happy except on an animal level. The happiness of *man* can only be achieved when he rises above his innate desires and strives for a goal beyond that of self-gratification. It is only then that he is a *mensch*. Failure to do so results in frustration, from which he seeks to escape by indulgence (the hedonistic treadmill) or by obtaining an artificial euphoria via brain-altering chemicals. Ironically, the true happiness of man is when he seeks the perfection of being a *mensch* by denial of many of his physical urges rather than by their gratification.

A human being becomes a *mensch* when he implements those potentials that are unique to man and which animals lack. In addition to greater intelligence, some of the more obvious uniquely human features are (1) the ability to learn from the history of past generations, (2) the ability to search for truth, (3) the ability to reflect on the purpose and goals of life, (4) the ability to have a self-awareness, (5) the ability to volitionally improve oneself, (6) the ability to have perspective, to contemplate the future, and to think about future consequences of one's actions, (7) the ability to be considerate of others and to be sensitive to their needs, (8) the ability to sacrifice one's comfort and possessions for the welfare of others, (9) the ability to empathize, (10) the ability to make moral and ethical choices in defiance of strong bodily drives and urges, (11) the ability to forgive, (12) the ability to aspire, and (13) the ability to delay gratification.

The sum total of all these uniquely human features constitutes the human *spirit*, and *spirituality* is the actualization of these potentials. According to this definition, non-spiritual man is nothing more than *homo sapiens*, an animal with intellect.

Many of the psychological and physical illnesses that afflict man are due to indulgence or escapist maneuvers. Indulgence is not restricted to sex, food, and drugs. A "type-a" person is ego-indulgent, on an ego-treadmill rather than a hedonistic treadmill. The development of *character*, which is nothing other than spirituality as defined, may eliminate many of the human afflictions that result from the frustration of being on a treadmill, exerting much effort, but never getting anywhere.

Holism has become a popular concept. It indeed refers to considering man as a unit rather than as an assemblage of parts, which the fragmentation of specialization has fostered. But considering a person as a physical unit, or even as a physical-psychological unit, is not yet really holistic. It is only when a person develops the character of spirituality that he becomes the complete being that God wished, and it is only when man is truly whole that he can achieve the happiness of being a *mensch*.

Chapter 2

But Will Good Character Pay My Bills?

Howard Jonas, *Founder and* CEO *of* IDT *Corporation*

On July 23, 1970, I pushed a makeshift hot dog stand to a street corner in the Bronx, in front of the Van Etten Hospital and across from a bar called the Tender Trap.

It's a shame that so many young people don't work. Instead they mooch off their parents, go to school, hang out, and consume indiscriminately, all the while finding time to criticize everyone else. We're all born naturally selfish. Only by enduring and overcoming life's hard knocks do we build our characters and become empathetic to other people's struggles. Working for a living forces us to learn to cooperate and to treat people right. Years ago, almost every young person had to work on the family farm, in the family store, or in some other job in order to make a necessary contribution to the family's survival. The character of previous generations was built from this sense of responsibility instilled from an early age.

What builds the character of youth today? Watching TV? Belonging to a gang? Playing on the high school golf team?

My character was built in a hot dog stand.

On Sunday mornings, the bar across the street was in a shambles. An elderly couple arrived early in a beat-up Dodge sedan to clean the place up. This was a big problem for me. I had a deal with the usual bartenders to supply me with ice during the week, and ice was the magical substance that fueled my business.

The secret to selling hot dogs is selling twice as many sodas. On every twenty-five-cent can of soda, I made fifteen cents, whereas on every twenty-five-cent frank I only made a dime. The hotter the summer day, the more I made, and in New York City, summer gets pretty sweaty. If the old couple refused to give me free ice, my profits would plummet. So I walked into the bar on my first Sunday prepared to negotiate, but when the old lady looked up from her mop, she just smiled and said, "Oh, you're the nice young man with the hot dog cart. Of course you can have ice; you can have whatever you like."

After that, we became friends. I offered her and her husband free hot dogs, but they were on a no-salt diet. I had started selling flowers, though (to the hospital visitors), so every Sunday when the old couple showed up, I crossed the street to get my ice, and brought the old lady the nicest rose I could find.

One Sunday morning, my hot dog, soda, and flower business came crashing down around me. Another vendor with a huge mechanized stand showed up with his twenty-four-year-old son to steal my spot. The vendor's son informed me that I had fifteen minutes to clear out or he'd come over and kick my you-know-what. Then he pulled a switchblade on me and said he'd kill me if I put up a fight.

Now on the one hand, I definitely didn't want to die. On the other hand, I wasn't giving up my spot.

I went over to the Tender Trap and asked the old lady to

call the cops if she saw anything happening to me. When I went back to my stand, though, the old lady came out behind me, screaming like a banshee. She told the father-son duo that it was my spot and they'd better leave if they knew what was good for them.

The father yelled back that he'd set up shop wherever he wanted, and called the old lady a terrible name. At that she turned around and went back inside the Tender Trap.

A couple of minutes later, three big Cadillacs (one pink and two white) screeched to a stop in front of our stands. Seven enormous men got out of the cars, and one of them charged the vendor screaming, "Who insulted my mother?" The vendor's son suddenly lost his bravado.

"Johnny," he pleaded, "I swear I didn't know she was your mother."

The old lady's son pummeled the younger man with two of his friends trying to restrain him.

"Calm down, Johnny. You don't want to kill the guy."

When Johnny finally calmed down, he told my competitors that if they brought their stand anywhere near my spot again, it would be the last day they ever sold hot dogs. He then took a baseball bat out of his trunk and bashed the chrome on their stand about eight or nine times to make sure they got the message. After that, I never saw them, or any other competitor, again.

When the other vendor took off, Johnny and his associates ordered hot dogs like they hadn't eaten for days. I assumed the dogs were on the house, fair compensation for services rendered, but Johnny not only insisted on paying, he gave me a twenty-dollar tip as well. When I refused, he told me it was for the flowers, and that "anyone who's a friend of my mother is a friend of mine, and I don't take no money from friends..."

Becoming friends with the old lady was probably the best business move I had ever made at that point in my blossoming career. But why exactly had I befriended her? Part of it was just that I needed to make sure I had a steady supply of ice. But more than that, I felt empathy for her and her husband. As I sat at my hot dog stand and watched them get out of their beat-up car to clean a filthy bar on the morning after a Saturday night rager, I could imagine myself in their shoes. They weren't rich, and it was obviously difficult to get up early in the morning, especially at their age, to clean out a bar. But they were independent. They worked hard and did the best they could, and I admired and respected them for that. Even at fourteen I realized that things don't always work out the way people intend – illness, business setbacks, bankruptcy, war, prison. You just never know.

In life, luck counts for a lot. I realized that I could be in their position in fifty years. This double awareness – that people should be judged on how much they do with what they're given, and not just on how much they accomplish; and also that given slightly altered circumstances, most other people in the world and I could easily have our roles reversed – has instilled in me a deep sense of humility.

Success in business, I think, comes as the result of a combination of many different factors, most of which can't be controlled. Talent and luck, for example, are God-given. Who knew Johnny would come to my rescue in his pink Caddy? The good news, however, is that good character, which is at least as essential, if not more so, to founding and running a major company, can be developed. Persistence, courage, patience, empathy, loyalty, honesty, integrity, kindness, generosity, the ability to cooperate with others – these can all be worked on and cultivated. Eventually most people, as they get older and work in the productive sphere, develop, out of necessity, into relatively decent people. Obviously it is a tremendous advantage, though, to form a good character and learn these values early on.

Of all these good character traits, though, humility is far and away the most important to develop if you want to succeed in business in a major way. Humility, that good character trait that saved my hot dog stand, serves me equally well as the CEO of a multibillion-dollar telecom company. Developing a sense of humility in my teens has literally made and saved me millions of dollars. Here's how…

In college, I ran one of the nation's most successful mail-order businesses. At that time, a lot of mail-order marketers were making big money selling small samples of well-known perfumes. I realized that the women ordering the samples had yet to commit to a single brand, and I also knew from my other businesses that people always wanted personalized products that were especially designed and made just for them. I hit upon what I thought was a brilliant idea: perfume personalized for your personality. Women would fill in a whole page of questions about their age, weight, favorite colors, dreams, pastimes, education, clothing preferences, etc…and we'd send them the perfect scent in the mail a few weeks later.

I even invented a fictional Italian perfumer, Giuseppe La-Verde, whom we featured in our ads as personally supervising the blending process for each fragrance. I was so enthralled with the idea, and the genius of my ads, that I could barely think of anything else. Estée Lauder, Charles Revlon, and Nina Ricci would soon be nothing compared to me.

Usually, when introducing a new product to the market, I ran a sample ad in a small publication before ordering any merchandise or placing a large advertising buy. This time, though, I was so sure of myself, and so anxious to launch my takeover of the cosmetics industry that I threw caution to the wind. I hired an expert fragrance chemist to formulate dozens of Giuseppe LaVerde perfumes so they would be ready when the orders came pouring in. I stocked my storeroom with cases and cases of the different perfume varieties. I spent $10,000 on a full-page ad in the *National Enquirer,* and sat back waiting to become rich beyond my wildest imagination.

But even my wildest imagination could not have conceived of the number of letters that would gush in for Giuseppe La-Verde. One. One single, thirty-three-year-old, green-eyed badminton enthusiast from Iowa filled out the survey and ordered her specially mixed scent. One! Giuseppe LaVerde had cost me over $25,000!

What Giuseppe and young Howard didn't yet know was that a woman wears perfume to be Lauren Hutton, Elle McPherson, or Coco Chanel, not to be herself – an overweight, middle-aged librarian with a degree from a junior college. How could I have been so stupid? What grandiosity! What recklessness! Mea culpa, mea culpa, mea culpa!

Eventually I learned my lesson, and I never ran an ad campaign again without testing it first. The rule has held true in every business I've been a part of since. Many times I've found that things I thought were sure bets weren't sure at all. When people are on a winning streak and think they're right, they often feel the need to put their money where their mouths are. You see this in Vegas whenever someone lets it all ride on black, or some quiet employee loses thirty years of savings on a risky investment. This kind of risk taking is pure hubris. There's always a way to test first, to gather information, to scope out competition, and generally to hedge the bet. Many of the most successful people in the business world *seem* to be big gamblers, but I promise you, they're never making bets that aren't well hedged.

Did any of history's great generals – Robert E. Lee, Alexander the Great, Hannibal – go into a battle and just "let it ride"? Without sending spies to gauge the enemy's capabilities first? Not a chance. Recently, Sun Tzu's *Art of War* has become popular (to display on bookshelves) among top corporate executives. These latter-day emperors, as they envision themselves, are brave, fearless risk takers battling a bunch of lily-livered office types. Or so they'd have you believe. The message conveyed by placing the book on the shelf is, "Watch your back around me. I'm a loose cannon."

If they actually took the time to read the book, they'd discover that Sun Tzu's main advice is to send out spies and do extensive reconnaissance work. In business this means keeping your nose to the ground, staying abreast of what the competition is doing, and testing even the surest of sure things, even if that means compromising the element of surprise in the marketplace. All this comes from a deep sense of humility. A businessman has to know he's fallible, that he's a human being who can and will make mistakes. Only a humble man has the discipline to avoid disaster by cutting his losses when he realizes he made a mistake. And only a humble man will really abide, year after year, by the business world's three most important rules: test, test, test.

Humility is also the key trait to possess if you want to inspire the people who work with you to put the full force of their hearts, souls, and creativity into your business. Many people who in other companies would have been pigeon-holed into lower-level positions were recognized at IDT for their vision, and rose to the top of the organization. Their contributions were critical to our success.

Whenever I hear someone from IDT say that he works for Howard Jonas, it sounds to me like fingernails scraping a blackboard. He works *with* Howard Jonas. For my part, I never say that anyone at IDT works *for* me, and this is not just some charade of modesty. It's how I really feel. We're all part of a team. I need the people I hire as much as they need me.

Journalists like to call me "one of the foremost innovators in the communications industry." The truth is that many of my best "innovations" were borrowed from suggestions I got from other people. I crave new ideas, and I love to be surrounded by creative people. More importantly, I try not to make snap judgments about who has something to teach me. What I've discovered is that it's possible to learn from everyone. Until you can look at any person, see him as an equal, and really listen to what he has to say, you'll never be sure whether he has something exciting to offer or not.

A former construction worker now manages over two hundred highly trained IDT technicians. One of our nighttime tech support supervisors figured out how to replace a huge multi-million-dollar mainframe online system with a few small PCs, which saved us millions. If you're humble (i.e., you don't think you're the only person with something to offer), you'll be able to tap into the brilliance of people all around you. For sure, not every suggestion is a winner, but then again, if you're not, as a rule, open to hearing other people's ideas, you don't even have a chance to profit from the great ones.

Humility is also at the core of my most successful hiring practices. Every growing business must overcome the problem of attracting and keeping great people. When IDT was just a start-up, I realized there were two categories of top people who might be willing to join my team. The first were those who simply chose the wrong career path. It's no harder to imagine a young person selecting an unsuitable profession than it is to imagine him marrying the wrong spouse. Who, after all, has any experience the first time they make one of these momentous decisions? A person can easily end up in an unrewarding job, where his potential is neither recognized, appreciated, nor fully harnessed.

The fact that a talented, energetic person makes a bad career choice in no way diminishes him as a person. Like a hardy blade of grass that cracks concrete to reach the sunlight, so will such a person's unrealized potential burst into view (for those humble enough to look). Show me a postman who in his spare time organizes, coaches, and runs a Little League team, for example, and I'll show you someone who could manage a large staff if he wasn't busy delivering the mail.

The second category of great people I recruited were those who chose the right field, started to succeed, but then crashed and burned. Big time. In fact, the more catastrophic the failure, the more certain I was that I'd found the right person for the job. Because generally it's the greatest undertakings, with the most talent and energy poured into them, that produce the most spectacular failures when something goes awry at the critical moment. I call this my spectacular failure theory.

In business, talent is no guarantee of success. Sometimes, you just need luck. Entrepreneurship requires a person to push into uncharted territories. There are going to be sensitive moments during the journey when, if the rope happens to snap unexpectedly, you're history. When this snap happens early in one's career (and due to the inexperience and daring of youth, this is precisely when failure is most likely to occur), it can be devastating, leaving a once high-flyer ruined and depressed.

What a great time to hire a guy. You can get him to come cheap, and he's eternally grateful (and loyal) to you for picking him up when he was down. Plus, what you've got on your team now is no ordinary shlepper, but a person of extraordinary vision and capability. Someone who can think and work independently. Someone with the ability to bring together and execute the different elements of a plan. Someone who knows how it feels to soar above the ordinary.

But he crashed and burned, you protest? So what, I retort. Who hasn't ever failed in his life? Only a person who never tried to do anything really difficult. An arrogant person with an inflated ego to defend will denigrate a spectacular failure so he can go on thinking that his success proves his inherent greatness. A humble person who hears the story of a spectacular failure realizes how easy it would be for the roles to be reversed.

My luck was better than theirs, or maybe I was just a little more cautious. Either way, to count the spectacular failures out in order to hold on to a delusion that my success resulted from some kind of innate superiority would have cost me some of my most valuable colleagues, including IDT's chief operating officer and mastermind, Howie Balter.

In order to hire the right staff, a CEO must also become acutely aware of his own shortcomings. The best part about working with other people is that they can compensate for your deficiencies and pick up the slack where you're weakest. The only reason IDT succeeds is because I work with a team of people who complement each other and cover for each other's inadequacies. Am I ashamed to admit that I need other people to help me run IDT? Certainly not. I know I'm not perfect. If I were, I wouldn't be human.

A company, however, can pursue perfection. Is the company lacking vigor? Hire young lions and set them free. Is it short on brainpower? Convince some real geniuses they'll be able to make their mark with you and create a brain trust. Are you short on stature and people skills? Maybe bring a former congressman on board. You can alleviate whatever shortcomings hold you back in the context of a great organization. But only if you're humble enough to admit that you're not omnipotent. History has watched the downfall of many leaders who surrounded themselves with lackeys and yes-men. Weak employees can make an arrogant CEO feel strong, but they won't help his company skyrocket to success in the long run.

When you realize that only a hair's breadth separates society's successes from its spectacular failures, and you see that being on top now in no way guarantees that you won't find yourself at the bottom in the future, you will probably want to help people who are less fortunate. If the roles were reversed, you'd want them to do the same for you. The irony is that charitability, which comes from humility, can have an extremely beneficial impact on the bottom line.

I started to give a lot of my income to charity in high school. At just that time, I became interested in my Jewish roots and discovered that the Jewish sages advise a person to give away between ten and twenty percent of his after-tax earnings. Twenty percent is the maximum because giving away more could endanger a person's financial stability, which would be bad for society as a whole. I therefore decided to try to give around twenty percent of my income to charity each year. It's hard to begin to relate how rewarding this decision has been.

First off, my charitable donations lift my self-image in ways nothing else can. Imagine how rich you feel when you can sit down and think about the truly needy people in the world, decide which ones you most want to help, and then send them a check that helps alleviate their suffering. I can tell you from experience that it makes you feel like a millionaire. It's just impossible to feel poor when you're giving away money. Charity also renders any luxury items you're "lacking" grossly unimportant. This is just as true when you live hand to mouth as when you live on Easy Street.

Giving money to those in need also keeps you balanced and pointed in the right direction. Instead of feeling envious and unhappy from having your mind focused constantly on people who have more wealth, talent, and accomplishments than you, you feel grateful and satisfied because of your awareness of those who have less. But most importantly, the tremendous sense of satisfaction that comes with supporting worthwhile organizations and charities motivates people who give to work hard, succeed, and earn more so they can give more.

When you think about it, doesn't it seem empty to channel all your creative powers into the pursuit of a Lexus? To me, it seems nuts. If amassing material possessions is truly the end goal of all the hard work, then maybe it would be better to stay home and read a good book. On the other hand, the people who come to work every morning in order to accomplish something noble, or to make the money needed to support a noble cause, wind up elevating their whole existence. Work is then transformed from a monotonous and mundane task to a spiritually uplifting and even sublime expression of your highest ideals. You don't just work to satisfy your own selfish desires, but to help others and make the world a better place.

One last thing. By getting involved in charitable organizations, you'll meet great people who may become your closest friends. Not only that, some of the people you meet will be extremely rich, important, and powerful. These people, who are totally inaccessible if you approach them in a business setting, are happy to talk to you at a charity board meeting. Who knows? One of these people might give you the venture capital money you need to pursue your dream. That's exactly what happened to me. I'm certainly not saying that you should get involved in these organizations in order to make good business connections. The only good reason to volunteer and support a charity is if you honestly believe in, and want to promote, their cause. But if the system is set up so that the contacts you make while doing the right thing help you in the business arena as well... well then, who am I to complain?

Chapter 3

The Cooperative Character

Professor Robert J. Aumann, PhD, *Winner of the 2005 Alfred Nobel Memorial Prize in Economic Sciences*

Repetition in strategic interactions leads to cooperation. In layman's terms, this means that you'll be nice to somebody today so that he'll be nice to you tomorrow. But of course, this only works when tomorrow is important to you today. If tomorrow isn't important to you today (i.e., if you are only concerned about the present moment, here and now), then you will only do what is good for you today. When tomorrow isn't important to you today, then the fact that the other guy isn't going to be nice to you tomorrow doesn't bother you all that much. In which case, you have no incentive to cooperate today, because what's usually good for you today is to look out for number one.

Said another way, if you want "peace now," you probably won't get peace now. But if you want peace later, you might just get peace now.

You're probably thinking, "How absurdly simple! For that they gave you the Nobel Prize?" Well, the editors of this volume asked me to make it simple, and I tried to comply with their wishes. This reminds me of a story in Sir Arthur Conan Doyle's *Sherlock Holmes*. Watson arrives at Holmes's study, opens the door, and Holmes is there leaning over his microscope. He looks up for a second and says to Watson, "I see you've decided not to invest in South African gold stocks." Watson is astounded. Holmes then proceeds to go through a whole long rigmarole of how he figured it out – takes up about half a page – because there was chalk on Watson's fingers, and that means he was at the club playing pool, and there was a certain gentleman Watson was sure to meet there who was bullish on South African gold stocks, and on and on. At the end of this long chain of deduction Watson cries out, "How absurdly simple!"

Sometimes the most important ideas are the "simplest."

The point, though, is that caring about the future – call it "patience" or "far-sightedness" – leads to cooperation.

Now this is not to say that Game Theory would call patience and far-sightedness inherently *good* character traits. Game Theory is an ethically neutral discipline and does not seek to evaluate or distinguish between good or bad. Patience is necessary for "success" in strategic interactions only if your goal is to foster cooperation. If you don't want cooperation in a given interaction or circumstance, then patience might be a very damaging character trait to possess.

Terrorists, for example, who blow themselves up on buses are successful and they are rational given their goals. Rationality means pursuing a strategy that is calculated to achieve your goals. A rational course of action is one that is in your best interest given the information you have at your disposal. Your goals may be to settle down, have a nice married life, and raise a family. But a terrorist probably has very different goals. That's not irrational. Terrorists are very rational, and they're achieving their short-term goal of getting the maximum media attention as well as their long-term goal of destroying the state of Israel. They're succeeding and they're very rational. Too often we confuse the word *rational* with "leading to desirable outcomes," or "good." Rationality isn't "good." Intelligence also isn't "good." We have all these ideas that we think about in positive terms, but they're not necessarily positive. Even cooperation isn't good in itself.

One of the most famous examples in Game Theory is the Prisoners' Dilemma.[1] We ask, "How can these two people achieve cooperation?" And we forget that these two people are both dangerous criminals! We don't want them to achieve cooperation!

---

1. Editor's note: For those not familiar with this game, the classic Prisoners' Dilemma is presented as follows:

   Two suspects, A and B, are arrested by the police. The police lack sufficient evidence for a conviction, and so, after separating the prisoners, visit each of them and offer the same proposition: if one testifies for the prosecution against the other and the other remains silent, the betrayer will go free and the silent accomplice will receive the maximum ten-year prison sentence. If both refuse to talk, both prisoners will only have to spend six months in jail. If each chooses to rat on his colleague, they'll both receive a two-year sentence. Each prisoner must make a choice – to rat out the other, or to remain silent. However, each must choose, given uncertainty about what the other prisoner will do.

	Prisoner B stays silent	Prisoner B betrays
Prisoner A stays silent	A = six months, B = six months	A = ten years, B = free
Prisoner A betrays	A = free, B = ten years	A = two years, B = two years

   Nonetheless, it turns out that it is always better (assuming that the prisoner's goal is to minimize his own stay in prison) to play the rat strategy. If his partner stays quiet, his best move is to betray as he then walks free instead of receiving the minor sentence. If his partner betrays, his best move is still to betray, as by doing so he receives two years as opposed to ten. Of course, his accomplice will likely come to the same conclusion.

We want the police to come out winning. The way this game is presented it's as if we're rooting for the prisoners to somehow achieve the "cooperate-cooperate" outcome. No! I want the police to win! At least usually. I suppose it depends who the prisoners are – they might be the people from Gush Katif.

At the core, Game Theory is about selfishness. Studying selfishness is not the same as advocating selfishness. Game Theory says nothing about whether the "rational way" is morally or ethically right. It just tells us what rational (i.e., self-interested) actors will do, not what they *should* do.

Game Theory recognizes those modes of behavior that we call "good character traits" as ways to foster cooperation in repeated interactions and to provide a person with an enhanced social existence. Game Theory can therefore explain why we might employ these character traits ("good" or not) even in situations where it seems there is no rational reason to do so – for example in a one-time interaction in a place where no one knows you, when you're unlikely to see this other person ever again (e.g., when you're driving through a remote area of Switzerland and the gas station attendant gives you back too much change). In such a case, a person may choose to maintain the behavior inherent in the good trait (honesty in this example) because having this trait as an internal need is ultimately a positive strategy in the long run. To always behave in ways that will protect your good name, even in situations where your reputa-

---

But when we reason from the perspective of the group (of two prisoners), the best strategy would be for both prisoners to keep quiet, as this will reduce their total jail time to one year. Any other decision will make them worse off when considered together. Thus we see that if the prisoners each act from self-interest, they will each end up with a worse fate than if each makes his decision based on what is best for the group as a whole.

tion is not threatened in any way, will in the long run be beneficial for a person in a social context, and will cause others to cooperate with him.

Another example: why do we leave tips in restaurants in foreign countries? You will probably never eat there again, and even if you do, you are unlikely to run across the same waiter, and even if you do, he is unlikely to remember that you stiffed him! A tip is a sign of gratitude and appreciation. In general when people are working for you, it's very important to encourage good work with a smile or a pat on the shoulder, or a financial reward. In fact, this is exactly what the Nobel Prize does. A person who accustoms himself to feeling a sense of gratitude, internally, will end up encouraging good work from those around him, and will earn a reputation that will motivate others to work with him.

Mark Twain in his famous *Harper's Magazine* article "Concerning the Jews" wrote that Jews are especially honest because the basis of successful business is honesty, since business cannot thrive where the parties don't trust each other. If you want cooperation, you have to keep your promises. The other side of protecting your reputation, though, is not letting other people break their promises to you.

In the Ultimatum Game, the experimenter gives subject A $100 to split between himself and B, who's somewhere off in another room. A makes an offer. If B refuses the offer, they both get nothing. Now we would expect the split to come out most of the time at around $90–$10. Maybe $80–$20. Because after all, getting $10 is better than getting nothing, right? But it turns out that B will reject most of the offers below $70–$30 or $60–$40. Is that rational? To walk away from a windfall of $20? We would tend to think not, but it is actually rational, because a person who gets a reputation for accepting bad deals won't get offered any good deals in the future. So even in this situation, where the participants are anonymous and playing a one-time game, it might make sense to maintain your internal standards and punish the other player for making you an unfair offer.

Now, Jewish thought expresses absolute truth and absolute values, since it expresses the truth that the Creator revealed. Still, it is worthwhile to see whether some aspect of that truth can be understood in terms of human thought. In that spirit, let us try to apply Game Theory to some Jewish ideas.

In Jewish thought, judging other people in a favorable light is considered to be a great virtue.

Why should this be an advantageous mode of behavior from a Game Theoretical perspective? Generally people seek to live up to expectations. It's a good idea to please others, because then they will try to please you. If you attribute good character to me, then you can benefit from my psychological need to please. If you expect me to cooperate and behave with good character, then if I do otherwise you will be disappointed. Since I usually try to not let others down, your expectations will motivate me to behave – at least towardss you – with good character. So it's highly beneficial to have what we call an *ayin tovah* (a good eye), which entails attributing good character to others, and thus practicing *dan l'kaf zchus* (i.e., judging them on the side of merit).

In the book of Exodus, we find the Jewish people trapped between the Red Sea and Pharaoh's swiftly approaching chariot army. In one of the most famous incidents in Tanach, G-d intervenes with a miraculous outpouring of loving-kindness, splitting the sea to give the Jews safe passage. Simultaneously, He unleashes rage and retribution on the Egyptians, ensnaring their chariots in mud, and violently drowning them in the churning waters. Unbounded love in one hand. Rage and retribution in the other. Both encapsulated within a single Being, and both expressed in a single moment. In the eighteenth century, Rabbi Eliyahu Kramer, known as the Vilna Gaon, wrote in his commentary to King Solomon's book of Proverbs that depending on the situation, a person might be called upon to react with tremendous kindness, or with very strict justice. In order to succeed in life, a person must therefore possess the ability to employ both modes of behavior in their extremes at the appropriate times. This was King Solomon's understanding of the ideal human character. Indeed, it was the character that G-d Himself displayed at the Red Sea.

Half a century of research in Game Theory has taught us that the ability to punish and to make credible threats leads to cooperation. In the Cold War, the nuclear arms race and the eventuality of mutually assured destruction kept the Americans and Russians at the negotiating table and away from the battlefield. As Teddy Roosevelt said, "Speak softly and carry a big stick..." This seems to be true at all levels of strategic interactions, from personal relationships to international negotiations; rational actors fare best when they have the ability to cooperate and also to punish.

In the realm of international relations, the prophet Isaiah anticipated this finding:

> In the end of days...the nations will say, let us ascend to the Mountain of the Lord, and He will teach us His ways.... He will adjudicate between nations.... They will beat their swords into shovels and their spears into harvesting shears. Nation will not lift up sword against nation, nor will they continue to learn war.[2]

---

2. Isaiah 2:2–4.

From a Game Theoretical standpoint, Isaiah was right on top of it. This situation of global peace and harmony only happens in the ultimate cooperative setup, when the nations of the world voluntarily go up to the Mountain of the Lord to have their disputes adjudicated. Only *then* should we disarm. Until then, we can hope and work for peace, but if our goal is to cooperate, we must continue to have weapons and the ability to wage war.

Chapter 4

Psycho-Neuro-Immunology: Health, Character, and Spirituality – the Science Connecting Body and Mind

Yakir Kaufman, MD, *Chairman of Department of Neurology at Herzog Hospital in Jerusalem*

When I was in medical school, my professors taught us every system in the body separately. We learned about the nervous system, the immune system, the endocrine system, etc., without much focus on the interactions between these systems. Since then, advances in medical technology have proven what we all intuitively know – that changes in one system cause changes in all the others. The body's various systems are interdependent – constantly interacting with and influencing each other.

We tend to want to look at the human body in a very simplistic way, but unfortunately it is not a simplistic organism. When we look at the body as a bunch of separate units without seeing the whole, we lose a lot of information that can be critical to helping patients maintain their health and protect themselves against future incidences of disease.

Studies in psycho-neuro-immunology show that changes in a person's state of mind can actually cause significant changes in the body. Most people know about the placebo effect, but why is it that a dummy pill can actually change the course of a devastating physical disease? Though science has yet to provide a clear answer to this question, the placebo effect is very real, and it tells us a lot about the power of the mind to profoundly affect the body.

A revolution in medical care is taking place as a result of increases in our understanding of cognitive neuroscience. One of the main players here is the limbic system, which is the center for emotions and also has a lot to do with memory and values. We understand how the limbic system works, and how the brain works, only because of relatively recent advancements in medical technology. Brain imaging, for example PET scans and functional MRIs, let us see how the mind functions – to know which areas in the brain allow us to see, to speak, and so on. Scientists now are looking even deeper into the emotional and spiritual activities of the brain. With functional MRI, we can actually map areas that are active in happiness, sadness, disgust, fear, anger, etc.

Molecular biology, which tracks how small quantities of molecules interact within cells, is the other frontier whose exploration is helping psycho-neuro-immunologists understand the complex interactions between the mind and the body. When molecules are secreted from the immune system, for example, they can go on to affect the nervous system and the endocrine system. For instance, the interleukins, which are secreted by the immune system, can go into the brain and actually change the functioning of the nervous system. To illustrate this, when a person has a flu virus, he usually experiences a change in his emotional makeup along with the physical symptoms. He's a little bit depressed, and his thought processes are a little dulled. This is all called "sickness behavior," and it happens as a result of the secretion of this substance, interleukin. When it reaches the central nervous system and the brain, interleukin causes prominent changes in a person's emotion and cognition.

How stress affects our physical health is one of the major focuses of psycho-neuro-immunology. As it is commonly used, *stress* is sort of an umbrella term for a lot of internal processes that we experience as inner turmoil, anxiety, sadness, anger, hostility, pessimism, feelings of social isolation, etc. These are only examples of feelings that trigger the physiological stress response in the body, which comes from an extraordinary demand on the psychological and physiological defenses and adaptor mechanisms, which in turn results in a neural-immune endocrine response.

Now, the main thing here is that many studies demonstrate the statistically significant correlation between stress and numerous disease states. These include heart disease, infectious diseases, cancer, hypertension, diabetes, allergies, immune-mediated diseases, gastrointestinal diseases respiratory tract infections…you name it; the correlations are demonstrated in the best medical journals in the world. And the number of these reports grows each year.

There are two arms of physiological responses to stress. The endocrine system (i.e., the hormones), respond by secreting cortisol, which is a hormone that goes into our bloodstream and affects almost every system in the body. Many cells in the body have a receptor for cortisol. The autonomic nervous system, specifically the sympathetic nervous system, responds by producing adrenaline, which also flows into the blood and affects almost all the organs and cells in the body. The consequence, when we have chronic secretion of cortisol and adrenaline, and thus chronic stress, is a very high level of wear and tear on the cells. When a person experiences stress, his arteries widen, his heart beats faster, the adrenal glands secrete, and the lungs ventilate faster. When I go to give a lecture, my kishkes are turning around, and it's all a function of the adrenaline and cortisol floating around in my bloodstream.

Acute stress is normal and important for life. If I didn't have an acute stress response I would just fall asleep at my podium when I give a lecture. But when people experience a *chronic* stress response, in which the stress response does not subside, or recurs frequently, then the wear and tear on the body becomes very damaging.

The cortisol in the blood inhibits the immune system, which means that when we are under stress, we are more susceptible to infection, our wounds heal more slowly, and we have a higher chance of getting cancer because the immune system is also responsible for killing the cancer cells in our bodies. The implication, here, is that understanding stress and how to manage it, mentally, is critical to our physical health.

Now this is interesting because stress management is primarily an issue of character development. For example, people who feel gratitude for what they have and don't feel entitled to the things they lack tend not to get angry. People who have less anger in their lives have less stress. Similarly, people who are less self-focused, who are more giving, and therefore have more and better relationships, tend not to suffer as much from anxiety and feelings of social isolation, which are also major triggers of the stress response. People who are humble can remain calm even if they don't get exactly what they want exactly when they want it. The list goes on and on, and the point here is that people who work on their characters – who prioritize personal development – can significantly reduce stress and improve their overall states of health and well-being.

Working on our characters becomes much more of a priority when we consider that the leading causes of mortality and morbidity in Western society are stroke, heart attack, and cancer. Cortisol, we know, has an important effect on atherosclerosis, clotting of the blood vessels, which is the underlying factor behind stroke and heart attacks. So stress is actually one of the major factors behind the leading causes of morbidity and mortality in Western society! Chronic stress can also cause gastric ulcers, irritable bowel syndrome, inflammatory bowel disease, gastric cancer, and so on. We also know that cortisol has an inhibitory effect on the sex hormones, including testosterone. This means that chronic stress, caused by bad character traits, negatively impacts a man's fertility.

One of the researchers now at the National Institutes of Health did a fantastic research study in the field of psycho-neuro-immunology that looked at levels of IgA (a protective immune factor against upper respiratory tract infections) in the saliva of medical students. The study concluded that levels of immunity go down towardss the end of the academic year, at exam time. And of course at that time the students suffer from more upper respiratory infections, more colds, and more flus. Stress and the general reduction of a person's psychological well-being can actually make an individual more susceptible to disease. The evidence is clear: if you have more stress you have more disease, and if you have less stress you can be healthier. And again, managing stress (and thus maintaining normal levels of immunity) really comes down to having good character traits. In the case of medical students, this means maintaining their good characters in the face of a tremendous workload and potentially serious consequences for sub-par performance, which is no small task even for the most refined human beings.

Usually when I speak in hospitals, I ask the students and doctors, "What is the definition of health?" and usually in a large crowd I may have at most three or four hands rising because we don't usually talk about this in medical schools. If we doctors cannot readily define what constitutes health, then how can we know if what we are doing enhances it?

The World Health Organization defines health as "a complete state of physical, mental, and social well-being." Now, this is right in line with psycho-neuro-immunology. Too often, though, we tend to think of health as merely the absence of disease and infirmity. Generally, Western medicine treats disease and infirmity. We are not usually trying to enhance our patients' physical, mental, and social well-being. In ancient China doctors had completely different incentives. They received their salaries from the government, and got paid when the people in their communities were healthy! When their patients were ill they would get less money, which created an incentive to practice preventative medicine, to enhance the well-being of patients, and to make sure they did not get sick to begin with. Western doctors' incentives work in just the opposite fashion. The more people are sick, the more surgeries we can perform and the more drugs we can prescribe.

When care ignores any aspect of the patient's being, he feels incomplete and this may interfere with healing physical problems. Studies in psycho-neuro-immunology have established that emotions like anxiety and hope can be factors in illness outcome. In many cases, the key to coping with serious illness and disability is a question of the patient's faith in a higher power, and a sense of spiritual well-being. Victor Frankl introduced the psychiatric community to the idea that the spiritual dimension cannot be ignored – that it is this aspect of ourselves that makes us uniquely human. So stress reduction and generally increasing our well-being, which includes improving our character traits and our spiritual well-being, can bring us to better states of overall health.

In 1994 the national Gallup Poll asked a sample of Americans if religion provides personal comfort and personal support. Seventy-eight percent answered yes. So spirituality is actually a major factor for the majority of people, even in Western society. A more recent national survey published in the *New England Journal of Medicine* showed that 90 percent of people turned to religion to help them cope with the 9/11 terror attacks. This demonstrates that spirituality is already a major way of managing stress in our modern "secular" society.

More than fifteen hundred medical studies have been conducted that show, not surprisingly, positive correlations between higher levels of spirituality/religiosity and health. *JAMA* published results showing that people with high levels of spirituality and religiosity have better adaptation to stress, more rapid remission from depression, and are better at coping with disease. The National Institutes of Health (NIH), which is maybe the most important medical research institution in the world, is funding more and more studies on the effects of spirituality and religiosity on health. One very good example was published in *Public Health,* and involved more than five thousand Californian adults who attended weekly religious services of some sort, and who were followed up for more than twenty-eight years. The study found that the death rate among these five thousand people with weekly religious attendance was almost half that of the general population. This is equivalent to people who exercise regularly and refrain from smoking.

So the effect of weekly religious attendance on mortality

(and this is a very large study) turns out to be quite prominent. An even larger study on more than twenty-one thousand
Americans concluded that people who have more than a weekly
attendance in religious services live seven years longer, on average, than their secular neighbors. Religiously active people have
longer life expectancies, and for black Americans the difference
is fourteen years!

People with higher levels of religious observance are also
more likely to survive heart surgery, and suffer from fewer heart
attacks. This data comes from a study of more than five hundred people and was published in the *International Journal of
Cardiology*. Another example – people with regular religious attendance have 40 percent less hypertension. Also, suicide rates
are four times lower for people who regularly attend religious
services. Other studies have shown that people with higher levels of spirituality have less depression and better compliance
to medical care. A national health population study of Canada,
with more than seventy thousand respondents, showed that
people with higher levels of spirituality have significantly lower
rates of stroke and migraines.

Preliminary findings in a study that we are conducting at
the clinic in Baycrest Hospital in Toronto, with sixty-eight Alzheimer's patients, suggests that patients with higher levels of
spirituality and religiosity have slower rates of progression of
Alzheimer's disease.

We already discussed the stress response, but on the opposite side of the coin is the relaxation response. Prayer, studies
show, actually elicits a relaxation response, which activates the
parasympathetic nervous system, lowers blood pressure, lowers heart rate, relaxes the muscles, and lowers digestive and
metabolic rates, which means that over time, the wear and tear
on the body is lower for people who pray regularly. I was in an

NIH conference about spirituality and health where Doctor Andrew Newberg presented results from PET scans which showed that significant changes take place in the brain while people are praying. Most of the action occurs in the superior parietal lobe, and also in the inferior parietal lobe. Researchers are becoming increasingly interested in the positive effects of prayer on the body and the mind. Recent studies even show that people who are prayed for actually have better health outcomes. This, of course, we can't explain scientifically, but nonetheless we observe that the effects of religious involvement on our health is profound on several levels.

On the one hand, religious people seem on average to have a number of behavioral and social advantages – like less smoking, less drinking, more and better marriages, and closer relationships with people in their communities. From a character perspective devoutly religious people also tend to be more charitable, more honest in their businesses, and to do more acts of kindness (e.g., visiting sick people in hospitals and bringing food to the poor). Religious people also report feeling more positive emotions, like hope and optimism, and less stress and anxiety, which in turn can have many physical health benefits, like less immune suppression, lower levels of stress hormones, less suicide, and better health outcomes.

These findings are cutting edge for medical science, but Jews have known about them for more than three thousand years. Every place you open the Torah you can find body-mind connections. Psycho-neuro-immunology is just illuminating, from a scientific perspective, one facet of the Jewish wisdom tradition. For example, the Rambam's principle that one must strive to have "a healthy mind and a healthy body" implies he was perhaps history's first psycho-neuro-immunologist! On a more esoteric level, Judaism understands that each part of the body corresponds to and symbolizes abstract ideas in the spiritual realm. The Maggid of Mezerich said that a small hole in the body is a large hole in the soul. And Rabbi Yitzchak Ginsburgh explains that "to heal the body we must first heal the soul."

At the root of our health problems are psychological and spiritual issues, and the process of dealing with them requires a more internal and more profound process. If we can address our patients' psychological/spiritual imbalances, we can actually affect their negative physical manifestations. And this is a more integrative and holistic approach. If we aim our treatments at the superficial symptomatic stages, then the root problem will just reroute and pop up again in a different place in a different form.

There was a very interesting study done by Griffin, looking at a health survey of more than seventy thousand Canadians who were grouped according to the following categories: people with high spirituality/religiosity, no spirituality/religiosity, high religiosity/non-spiritual, and high spirituality/non-religious. Dr. Griffin found that the highly spiritual and religious group had better health outcomes in terms of mental health and overall well-being than the rest. One of the more interesting results emerging from these studies is that it's not enough just to be spiritual or just to be religious, but that real inner well-being and health come from being religious in a spiritual way.

All this points to the fact that our health is just one of many outward expressions of who we are internally – like the way we dress, the way we talk, our handwriting, and our facial expressions. If we can find ways to develop ourselves internally, so that we can become genuinely more caring, generous, humble, grateful, honest, faithful, spiritually sensitive people, then our more positive and more beautiful internal selves will manifest externally as fit, healthy bodies.

Chapter 5

Creating the Jewish Voice

Malcolm Hoenlein, *Executive Vice-Chairman
of the Conference of Presidents of Major
American Jewish Organizations*

*The Conference of Presidents of Major American Jewish
Organizations is the central forum for organized American Jewry
on vital issues of international and national concern. Representing
fifty-two national Jewish organizations, the conference provides a
common voice for affiliated American Jews from across the political
and religious spectrum, forging diverse groups into a unified
force for Israel's well-being, and for protecting and enhancing the
security and dignity of Jews at home and abroad. It brings together
American Jewish organizational leadership, key American, Israeli,
and other world leaders to address issues of critical concern to the
Jewish community.*

*Publicly, and even more so behind the scenes, the conference,
together with its member agencies, takes the lead in promoting
the interests of the American Jewish community and fostering the
understanding that a safe and secure Israel will continue to be
America's vital strategic ally and partner.*

* * *

Consensus is a rare and elusive creature, and finding it – hidden amongst outspoken, powerful, and passionate Jewish leaders – continues to be one of the greatest challenges of my job as the Executive Vice-Chairman of the Conference of Presidents of Major American Jewish Organizations. To succeed, the conference must consistently bridge the wide chasms that separate orthodox and reform, liberals and conservatives, hawks and doves – to bring these diverse groups together under the banner of "American Jewry." At times, creating a harmonious, unified Jewish voice to present to the world out of the cacophony of differing perspectives has seemed like an impossible task. Effective management of such a widely varying and potentially volatile organization, in order to promote Israel's interests and those of the Jewish people as a whole, requires the successful deployment of a whole host of character traits and interpersonal skills. Of them, the three I think are of the greatest value to me on a daily basis at the conference are (1) what Jews call *ayin tovah*, or the ability to see and appreciate the good in other people, (2) the ability to listen well, and (3) sincerity.

As Moses' successful forty-year term as the leader of the Jewish people came to an end, God chose Joshua to replace him at the helm. The Torah records that he was the most fitting successor for Moses because he was considered to be a man "in whom there is *spirit*."[1] Rashi, the eleventh-century commentator, explains that this unusual description alludes to Joshua's exceptional ability to connect to, and deal well with, many different kinds of personalities. Apparently this character trait topped the list of sought-after qualities in the chief executive who would ultimately shepherd the Jews across the Jordan and into the Land of Israel.

---

1. See Numbers 27:16–18.

If an organization hopes to function at its maximum level of performance, each member must willingly and enthusiastically contribute his energy and talents towardss the cause. It is indeed remarkable that thousands of years after Joshua galvanized the first Jewish army to fight and win the battle of Jericho, my experience at the conference still suggests that a leader's most critical attribute is his ability to recognize each individual's special brand of greatness.

Most people only really appreciate the talents that they themselves possess. People who pride themselves on their intelligence tend to value intellect in others. Especially kind people usually connect well with others who seek in all interactions to be givers. To effectively motivate a diverse collection of people to use their gifts in the service of the organization's goals, a good leader has to develop an appreciation for the qualities each member has to give – or else he will overlook opportunities and waste his most precious human resources. It takes broad vision, insight, and a certain degree of humility to see that group members whose skill sets are very different from one's own are able to contribute in meaningful ways. Unfortunately the job doesn't stop at recognition; an effective leader must also find the means to draw out and channel members' untapped potential in ways that are helpful to the organization.

In Jewish literature, this mixture of highly refined interpersonal skills is grouped together under the term *ayin tovah* – a "good eye." When a leader possesses an *ayin tovah*, the people around him feel that he senses their potential for greatness and that he wholeheartedly wants them to give expression to their virtues (i.e., that he genuinely cares about them). As a consequence, people trust this kind of leader, want to cooperate with him, and want to bring out their best efforts to help his organization accomplish its goals.

Maintaining a belief in the presidents' desire to work together to find common ground, in spite of their obvious differences, is a major part of consensus building at the conference.
The biblical figure Aaron, the first Jewish high priest, was re-
nowned for his ability to make peace between arguing factions,
particularly husbands and wives. His primary strategy for re-
solving marital disputes was to approach the parties separately
to "inform" them that the other really wanted to make up. As
a result, when the couple met to discuss their grievances, they
came to the negotiating table with a sense of goodwill and a
spirit of reconciliation. At the heart of this somewhat risky conflict resolution strategy is a particular *ayin tovah* – namely, a
belief in the underlying desire of most people to live and work
together harmoniously. The men and women at the conference
selflessly dedicate their time and energy in order to contribute
to the well-being of the Jewish people. Remembering that their
positions all emanate from a common core – the sincere desire
to do what is best for Israel and for the Jewish world – is what
keeps consensus, however elusive, always within reach.

A man once came to a famous rabbi just before Passover
to ask if he could substitute milk for wine in his four cups at
the Seder. Immediately this rabbi took out his wallet and gave
the man a wad of cash – enough money to buy a few bottles
of wine and a chicken to serve with the matzah at the holiday
meal. When the man left, the rabbi explained to the befuddled
students who witnessed the interaction that the man obviously
needed money for wine or else the question never would have
arisen. And if he specifically wanted to replace the wine with
milk, then he must have needed money to buy meat too (because
Jewish law prohibits eating milk and meat during the course of
a single meal).

Frequently, the key to finding a compromise between two

seemingly opposite positions is the ability to listen well. Listening well, as this story illustrates, often means discerning what facts and assumptions lie concealed behind a person's words. To locate the point of commonality (that desire to make a positive contribution to the Jewish people) in conference members' opposing views, one must constantly seek to understand the vantage points from which their policies stem. When one really understands where the other side is coming from, it usually makes perfect sense why they think their policies will be successful. Too many times, we debate to try to change other people's minds at a very shallow level. Should the US be at war in Iraq? Should the Fed raise interest rates? Should Israel be allowed to build its security fence? The "yes" and "no" answers that resound from the various sides of these debates are too infrequently backed up by serious discussions about the assumptions that give rise to the various opinions. If a leader hopes to build consensus, he must always listen for the vantage point. To get someone to recognize that his underlying assumptions don't take certain facts into account is usually a much smoother route of persuasion than trying to convince him that his well-reasoned and well-intentioned policies will do more damage than good.

Unfortunately, finding a fragile consensus and keeping it intact is only the beginning of the process. Once the conference formulates its position on a particular issue, we must then communicate our message, selling it effectively to the media and decision makers whose choices profoundly affect the Jewish world. This job requires clarity of thought, eloquence, passion, persistence, a command of history and politics, and most of all sincerity. Scores of volumes have been written about how to communicate effectively, how to persuade, spin, manipulate, and sell. Many of these techniques must work, because after all, the authors continue to convince buyers to pay for their books.

In my experience, though, people in positions of real power, particularly in Washington, catch on to salesmen who try to tell them what they want to hear. Politicians, especially, have an acute sensitivity to persuasion tactics as they have to employ them with voters all the time. A famous saying from the Jewish people's oral wisdom tradition relates that *devarim hayotzim min halev, nichnasim el halev* – "words that emanate from the heart, enter the heart." Sincerity works. In all my dealings with politicians and reporters around the world, I find this to be true time and time again. If a person wants to convey a message, let him first believe in it deeply, and be committed to fighting for it. Then he can deliver his words with the force necessary to cut through all the noise generated by opponents, and to penetrate the jaded hearts and minds of those he seeks to inspire.

There are many people who work selflessly and tirelessly to ensure the Jewish people's survival, but who nonetheless never stop to ask why it matters whether or not there are Jews in the world at all. The Conference of Presidents of Major American Jewish Organizations works on behalf of the Jewish people because we believe that we Jews have a mission to fulfill on this planet – namely, to be a light unto the nations. Practically, this entails sharing the most advanced systems of ethics and justice ever devised, and promoting the modes of behavior and perception that constitute truly "good character." More and more, I think the medium is the message. To promote our national interests effectively in a context that grows more turbulent and uncertain every day, we have to engage each other and the world with ever increasing levels of refinement. As we cooperate to unite and form consensus despite our rifts, we demonstrate to the world that it is possible to resolve deep-seated conflicts and work together without aggression or offense. So too, as we succeed without the help of dirty tricks, we demonstrate to the world that the marriage of truth and passion generally prevails. It might even be fair to say that all the great successes we've achieved at the conference on behalf of the Jewish people are really just the rewards for having developed good character – for always seeking to build unity, and for dealing openly and honestly with everyone we meet.

Chapter 6

The Song of the Soul

Rabbi Dovid Gottlieb, PhD, *former professor of mathematical logic at Johns Hopkins University, and senior lecturer of Jewish Philosophy at Ohr Somayach in Jerusalem.*

I. EXPLORATION

Character is a matter of universal interest. Parents are concerned with the character development of their children. Psychologists try to create strategies that will aid parents and children in this endeavor. Political contests are often decided largely on the perceived characters of the candidates. Biographies and novels explore the depths and subtleties of human nature. Human resource departments of companies try to assess the character of a job applicant. And every individual, from time to time, notices aspects of his own character, some of which please him, and some of which need improvement.

The whole subject would benefit from some general clarification. There are fundamental questions that lie behind our interest in character, but that rarely are asked. What is good character? Which particular traits are good and which not? What combinations of traits create good character as a whole? And why is good character important? Is good character important only because it leads to good actions, or is it important in itself? If the latter, how does good character bear on the goodness of actions?

There is no accepted secular position on good character with answers to these questions. Indeed, in a world that takes seriously the possibility that there are no real values or moral absolutes, it is hard to imagine such a position that would be generally acceptable. I suggest that we explore our own intuitions. We will examine a number of scenarios and observe our feelings about them. Then we will look at the Jewish explanation for those feelings. That will lead to answers to some of the questions.

#1 The Surgeon

Phillip qualified in surgery and developed a series of new operations with unprecedented benefit for certain crippling and fatal conditions. He made detailed videotapes of his operations and made them available to medical schools at no charge. He trained students to perform his new surgery. In addition, he did operations gratis for patients too poor to pay the fee. The community naturally thinks of him as a wonderful person, and we share their feelings.

Now imagine we discover that a secret foundation has been paying him for all his "good deeds." Millions of dollars have been deposited in a secret Swiss bank account as compensation for each of his "generous" actions. Phillip is investing this money in his retirement, which he plans for age fifty-five, after which he will stop doing surgery and devote himself solely to his pleasures. Does this not drastically change our feeling about him? Instead of seeing him as generous, sympathetic, and public spirited, we see him as (largely) selfish. His motivation reveals the character behind his actions – a character much less admirable than we thought.

It may be suggested that our change in attitude towardss Phillip is due at least in part to the fact that now we now cannot expect the continued benefit of his actions after age fifty-five. How can we reveal our feelings concerning his character, independent of his actions? Here is how: let us imagine that in fact Phillip dies at age fifty-four, and the information about his selfish motivation becomes known only after his death. The information affects only how we feel about the actions he performed while he was alive, even though in this case we have no expectations for continued benefit. Still it seems that our feelings will change.

And now suppose – a second possibility – that we discover Phillip has been hypnotized. All his "good deeds" were the result of posthypnotic suggestion. He could not have done otherwise – he had no choice. Does this not eliminate entirely our positive evaluation of his "good deeds"? In this case they are not even selfish, they are merely "programmed." No "character" at all is involved in his actions. And again, we may imagine that this information comes to light only after his death. So the value of his actions to the community while he was alive is not affected by the information. And yet our feeling changes.

What we see is that looking at actions "from the outside" does not reveal their true nature, and certainly does not reveal the nature of the person performing the actions. When we see the motivation "inside," our feelings change, even though the difference in character on the "inside" makes no difference to the effects of the actions at all.

#2 Altruism

It is January 3 in Chicago and it is sleeting. Your car engine has stopped on the highway. It will take the service truck an hour to reach you. A passing motorist notices you and stops to offer his help. He happens to be an auto mechanic. He looks under the hood, makes a few adjustments, and your motor is running again! Before you can even thank him he jumps back in his car and drives away. [Snow covers his license plate so you cannot see the number...] You are very grateful – and impressed. He took the time, stood in the sleet, fixed your car, and received nothing in return – not even your gratitude.

As you tell this experience to a friend, he remarks that you are very naïve. How do you think your benefactor felt as he drove off? He felt satisfied, proud of himself, and happy. And how would he have felt if he had not helped you? Small, mean, petty – and guilty. Look at the payoff for his fifteen minutes in the sleet: considerable pleasure, and avoiding considerable pain. What we naively call altruism is simply another calculation of benefit in terms of personal pleasure and (avoiding) personal pain. There is no such thing as real altruism – everything we do is done only for the sake of personal benefit.

Who is right? You, with your feeling of gratitude for your helper's altruism, or your friend who sees all actions as selfish? You are right, and here is the reason. Your friend is confusing the by-products of an action with its reasons. Yes, your helper gained pleasure and avoided pain by his action, but it does not follow that those were his *reasons* for acting. Altruism is determined by the reasons for the action, not by the by-products. And while it is true that sometimes we may have some selfish motivations, we also have some altruistic motivations.

Here is an example that will illustrate the difference between by-products and reasons. A fire breaks out at the local art museum. Henry, an art student, is passing by. Horrified at the imminent destruction of so many works of great art, he rushes inside and rapidly removes as many paintings as possible. This takes him two hours of very strenuous effort. A week later we ask Henry whether he thinks that the effort increased his muscular strength. He answers realistically that he believes it did. Now imagine suggesting to him that that is the only reason he did it – he removed the paintings in order to have a good workout and strengthen his muscles. That is ludicrous! Increased strength was a beneficial by-product of his deed, but not even part of the reason he did it.

In addition, the fact that he did strengthen his muscles does not detract from his altruism at all. We do not think less of his action when we realize that it made him stronger. An altruist is someone who acts for another's benefit. What makes him an altruist is that his reason for acting is to help the other person. Nothing prevents the altruist from receiving a benefit from his actions, as long as the benefit was not his reason for acting.

Similarly, when your friend attacks your helper's altruism by using the fact that your helper received benefit from his help, he needs to show that the benefit was your helper's reason for acting. He has done nothing to show that. Yes, whenever the altruist is successful in his efforts to help he will benefit. At the least, he will have the satisfaction of having succeeded in his effort to help. But no, that does not undermine altruism, since we have no reason to suppose that the benefit is the reason for his action.

It is true that Henry was very likely unaware of the benefit to his strength, while your benefactor may well have been aware of the satisfaction he would achieve, and the guilt he would avoid, from helping you. But the fact that he knew the benefits would occur does not mean that they were his reason for acting.

A person can be aware of benefits and yet not be motivated by them, or at least not be motivated *solely* by them. Think back to Phillip, the surgeon. When he receives payment for surgery he knows that he is receiving a benefit. But the fact that he does surgery on other occasions without payment indicates that he has other motivations for doing surgery. Even if the payment does *partly* motivate him, it is not his *sole* motivation. So we still have no reason to think that his motivation is wholly selfish.

If we look a little deeper, we will see that your friend has made another mistake. Let's ask why your helper felt pleasure in helping you, and why he would have felt pain at passing you by. After all, not everyone feels that way. Some would feel no pleasure in helping and no guilt in passing you by. Others would feel the pleasure and the guilt, but so weakly that they too would pass you by. What explains the difference between their feelings and those of your helper?

Obviously it is something in their psychology, in their motivations, that causes those differences. Your helper is the kind of person who feels a strong duty to help others, and has a strong desire for others to be helped. So, when he has an opportunity to help, his sense of duty and his desire for others' benefit lead him to act. The others do not possess the same strength of duty and desire.

Now when his efforts are successful, his actions give him the pleasure of duty fulfilled and desire satisfied. If he had passed you by, then duty and desire would have been frustrated – that is the source of the pain he would have felt. His sense of duty and desire for your benefit are what motivated his action. Duty and desire lead directly to the action. The pleasure and avoidance of pain were by-products.

The others would pass by without any thought at all, or with minimal feelings of guilt. Seeing others in distress bothers them only a little, if at all. They would derive little pleasure and avoid only little pain by stopping to help because they lack the strong sense of duty and desire that motivated the helper. We see (again) that the difference lies in the motivations of the two people, and the pleasure/avoidance of pain for the helper is the by-product of his [successful] action of duty and desire to help.

In sum, whether an action is altruistic depends upon the reason for the action. Altruism is a matter of the acting out of a certain inner character.[1] Our interest in altruism is an interest in character.

---

1.   This discussion is the tip of a philosophical iceberg. The critic will ask whether we can do what your friend cannot – can we show that the pleasure he receives is not his reason for acting? After all, the case of increased strength is very artificial. The mechanic surely knew that he would feel satisfaction as a result of his action, and that he would have suffered if he had not helped. Can we show that even in such a case the pleasure and avoidance of pain is a by-product of the action?

The answer lies in a famous argument of the British philosopher Bishop Joseph Butler. I cannot do justice to the argument here, but the following is an overly brief expression of the idea: "satisfaction" is the pleasure we derive from a desire achieving its object. There are cases in which the only pleasure available is a pleasure of satisfaction. In such a situation we must have a desire for something other than pleasure, and the pleasure we receive is a by-product of the action.

The critic will also want to know why altruism is a virtue, why it is admirable, if it is determined by a sense of duty and a desire. Are those aspects of character not merely motivations that cause his action? Is the helper not a prisoner of his motivations and thus not worthy of credit for them?

In the literature there are two answers to this question. One: motivations do not strictly cause actions. (This is the position of John Searle.) Two: motivations can be created by judgments of value, so that even if they do cause actions, the person himself is the cause of the formation of those motivations. (This is the position of Thomas Nagel.) So the critic should understand that his question is relevant, important, and that it has answers.

These scenarios illustrate a general perspective on human action. An action is not merely the motion of a body with its attendant effects. It is essentially an expression of character. To take a brutal example, there is a world of difference between the accidental explosion of a gas main, on the one hand, and a suicide bomber on the other. In both cases people may be killed and injured by an explosion. But only the latter is an action. Part of the difference lies in the fact that the suicide bomber has a goal and a conception of the world that together lead to the motions of his body. The gas main has neither, obviously.

I remember during the Vietnam War, when students were taking over street intersections and public buildings, that there were two groups pushing for brutal repression. One was the far right who wanted to teach the students a lesson. The other was the far left who were hoping that the brutal repression would spark a revolution. Now when you observe the votes in the city council in favor of repression, you cannot appreciate each vote as a complete human action unless you know (at least) to which camp the voter belongs.

What we see is that the character behind the action is part of the essence of the action. Understanding actions automatically includes understanding character. The challenge of the biographer and the historian is to take external events, most particularly human actions, and reveal their true human essence by filling in the character behind the actions. Without that background all we have is happenings, not actions.

#3 Duty vs. Love

A man has two sons. He raised both of them with great love, devotion, sensitivity, and sacrifice. Both are respectful, and both attend faithfully to their father's needs. The first does so out of duty. He finds helping his father difficult, painful, irritating, and exhausting. But he knows it is the right thing to do, so he does it. He even puts on a cheerful face so that his father will not know his true feelings. The second son loves his father so much that for him the opportunity to do something for his father is a great pleasure. He feels happiness, inspiration, and joy in serving his father.

How do we feel about the service of the two sons? The father benefits the same way from both. Still, there is something more impressive in the second son, something more noble, more ideal. Imagine that, at the end of his life, the father discovers the truth about the motivation of the first son. Will this not be a great disappointment? Would not the father prefer to be served out of love rather than out of grudging duty?

And notice that this feeling runs counter to another very natural feeling about generosity. Usually we feel that the more the generosity costs the giver, the more it is worth. A loan from a person of modest means is a greater act of generosity than the same loan from a wealthy person. The former deserves more gratitude than the latter. And in our case, the first son has to overcome much discomfort to perform his service, while the second son derives great pleasure from his service. From the point of view of cost, the service of the first son ought to be more valuable. And yet our feeling runs in the opposite direction.

Our feeling seems to be that the service of the second son expresses a difference in character, and that the extra cost paid by the first son does not offset the second son's superior character. Let us notice in this case that both sons are good people. The actions of both are morally praiseworthy. In fact, it is not clear that the *actions* of the second son are superior. It seems that we feel him to be a better person "in his essence," we might say. Part of our feeling stems from the first son's lack of gratitude for his father's loving care. It seems that his father's love left him cold – the son seems base, almost unnatural. He seems to suffer from a kind of moral blindness that bespeaks a deformed, degraded character.

Notice also that, if we take the second son as our ideal, performing well morally need not involve pain, suffering, deprivation, and so on. With the right character, a morally ideal life might be filled with pleasure and joy.

As a variation on this theme, think about how we feel about crimes. X steals five hundred dollars from Y. When we evaluate the crime, it makes a great difference who Y is. Y might be a stranger to X, or X's employee, or X's friend, or someone who saved X's life…We may assume that the loss of five hundred dollars affects each person in the same way. And suppose that Y does not know that X is the thief. Still, the crime gets worse as we progress down the list. That is because the character of X is worse in the successive cases. His lack of justice and gratitude show more meanness and corruption. So our feeling varies with our assessment of the character behind the action.

#4 Effort/Accomplishment

You meet Phyllis when she is twenty-four years old. She strikes you as exceptionally sensitive to others. She also exudes an air of calm self-possession. You find these traits very admirable. You take her as a model of how you would like to develop.

Now two possibilities. One: You discover that she has always been that way. She was a placid newborn, crying and fussing only on a rare occasion (there really are babies like that!). And when she heard other babies crying, she also cried. This is natural for all babies, but Phyllis cried more. Throughout her childhood, and up to the time you met her, these traits manifested themselves consistently.

Or two: As a child Phyllis was nervous, aggressive, and selfish. As a result, her relationships with her peers and with adults were troubled. At age seventeen she decided this should not continue and undertook a course of counseling that lasted four years. After great effort, and considerable pain, she succeeded in forming the traits you observed.

How do our feelings differ concerning the two possibilities? Do we not feel more admiration for the second? Let us imagine that from age twenty-one onwards the two possibilities are identical – Phyllis lives the same life in both. Her struggle to improve her character has no further effects on her life.[2] The difference in feeling still remains.

It is natural to feel admiration for accomplishments and not for (or not as much for) natural gifts. Why? Part of the answer seems to be that accomplishments often reveal admirable traits of character and that makes the difference. It is not that her being sensitive and focused is more valuable in the second case. In terms of their value for her and for others the two cases may be equal. Rather, in the second case she is a greater person.

There is a theme that runs through the examples. It is not on the surface, but if we probe, we can see it. The theme is love. In each case, what we respect, value, treasure, cherish in the ideal condition is the expression of loving. Let us review the examples.

What motivates a surgeon to work often for no pay, to make his innovative surgery available to the world again and again without recompense? He is giving freely of himself to help improve the health of as many people as he can. We take that as an expression of his love for people generally. We understand that he shares the pain of the ill and injured and rejoices at their

---

2. If this is too hard to imagine, we can simply imagine that you meet her immediately after the accomplishment and then she dies.

recovery. His empathy and identification with them expresses his love.

We can test this analysis. Let us try another variation on the story. As a child Phillip, the future surgeon, loses a very close friend to a botched surgery and is scarred for life. At first he simply hates surgeons. As he matures, his hatred leads him to a practical plan: he will drive incompetent surgeons from the profession by so raising the standard of surgery that they will no longer be employable. This is what motivates all his medical dedication. Does not this new scenario revise our feelings for Phillip? His actions are still good. But now they are motivated by hatred rather than love. This makes his actions, and his character, less admirable. I think this is a general observation: any variation we imagine that changes the motivation from love to something else will cause our evaluation to go down.

The same is true in the second example, of the auto mechanic on the snowy highway. Altruism is a large part of love. The ability to care for the other, to act for the other is an indispensable part of love. That is part of the reason that the suggestion that the actions of the helper are all selfish strikes us as more than merely wrong, but actually dangerous. It strikes at our understanding of a fundamental part of our humanity, the capacity to love. A being incapable of altruism would be incapable of love, and would thus not be really human.

In the third example, the two sons who serve their father with differing attitudes, the element of love is on the surface. The central difference between the two sons is the sensitivity to the love of the father, and the capacity and will to respond in kind. The dutiful son seems humanly crippled in his incapacity to love.

The fourth example is perhaps the most difficult to analyze. Phyllis is loving in her relationships in both scenarios. The only difference is what makes her so, outside causes or her own efforts. Still, I think there is a difference in terms of love, namely, her motivation to make the effort to change. At age seventeen, when she decided that she could not continue her nervous, aggressive, and selfish behavior, why did she decide? Was it the simple observation that her life had much pain, and that those with more loving relationships got more pleasure out of life? Or was it the perception that life without love is subhuman, that an essential part of her was not living? Do not the two possibilities affect our estimation of her efforts? The motivation to relieve her pain, while wholly appropriate, does not express nobility. The motivation to become a loving person elicits our admiration. One way to see this is to ask what would be appropriate for Phyllis to sacrifice in order to change her character. If it is a matter of increasing her pleasure and reducing her pain, the calculation will be made in terms of how the bottom line comes out: how much pleasure will be lost by the investment of so much time, money, and effort to change vs. the expected improvement in the pain/pleasure ratio as a result of the change. If it is a matter of developing an essential part of her humanity the decision will be made in other terms. In particular we expect that a greater investment of lost pleasure would be justified than the first calculation would tolerate.

The upshot of our discussion is this: an essential element in the ideal life is love, both the capacity to recognize love in others and the capacity to respond or initiate out of love for others. This is a key element in our appreciation of good character.

#5 Building Character

A Jew came to a rabbi and said that he had been deathly ill. His recovery was miraculous and he wanted therefore to give four hundred rubles to charity. He left the money with the rabbi. The next person to approach the rabbi said that he had found a suitable match for his daughter, but the expense of the match was four hundred rubles – money that he did not have. The rabbi said to himself: "I just received four hundred rubles for charity, and the next person needs exactly that sum. This cannot be an accident." So he gave the four hundred rubles to the second man.

A few minutes passed. The rabbi called his secretary and told him to find the man and bring him back. When he entered, the rabbi told him to put the money on the desk and go outside and wait. After two hours he called the man back and gave him the money and let him go.

The secretary was mystified. Obviously the rabbi had a good reason to give the money to the second person. What had caused his doubt, and how had he resolved it? The rabbi explained, "After the man left I had the sudden thought – don't give all the money to one person. Let many people benefit – split it up! And then I realized that of these two thoughts – to give it all to the second man, or to split it up – one came from my good side (*yetzer tov*) and one from the bad (*yetzer hara*). I had to discover which was which."

The secretary asked "So how did you figure it out?" The rabbi answered, "The second thought – to split up the money – came from a negative source: '*Don't give* the money to one person...' A thought whose source is 'Don't give' comes from the bad side. That is why I chose the first thought."

This is a challenging story. Did you guess the ending? I think most people would try to calculate the benefits to the recipients. Perhaps splitting the money creates more benefit (think of the "marginal utility of money"). Perhaps the need for a dowry outweighs other needs. And so on. The rabbi's decision was determined by the psychological source of the thought. How are we to understand this?

Here is a start, built on the feelings we shared in the prior scenarios. Thoughts and actions have psychological roots. When a thought leads to an action, the root is strengthened. When we decide against the action, the root is weakened. In other words, actions have internal effects as much as they have external effects. They affect our character. So in deciding what to do, we have two types of considerations – what difference the actions will make to the world external to ourselves, and what difference the actions will make to ourselves.

The rabbi was looking at the internal side. We do not know what he thought about the external side. Here there is a need for deep soul searching. He found the answer in the seemingly trivial phraseology, "Don't give." The negative in "Don't give" meant that the source of the thought was in withholding, as against the first thought, which was rooted in giving. The rabbi knew that it was wrong to reinforce withholding, and thus rejected the second thought. We could speculate: suppose the second thought had come phrased differently? Say, "There are so many people in need – I should give the money to more people." In that case perhaps the rabbi would have decided differently.

What this story illustrates is the necessity of taking responsibility for our character development. And I mean "necessity" in a very strong sense here. The effects on character are going to happen automatically. We cannot avoid them. Another evening in front of the TV, feet up, beer and pretzels within reach is going to reinforce laziness and self-indulgence. Another stiff competition at doubles tennis is going to reinforce aggression and competitiveness. An evening of cooperative effort for charity or visiting the ill will have very different effects on our character.

It is true that in this case the effects on character will also (usually) impact on future actions. But that is not the only reason to be concerned. As we saw from the previous scenarios, we care about character for itself also.

If we take the impact of our actions on our character seriously, it will have an important affect on our decisions. I need exercise. Mountain climbing and doubles tennis are my options. Knowing my propensities for aggression and competitiveness, I may choose the mountain. Or, if I can, I may specifically choose the tennis, and try to play a different sort of game – with sensitivity and generosity. I asked a second-year law student what kind of law he was expecting to practice. He answered that he had always wanted litigation since he was gifted at debating – fast thinking, precise expression, theatrical delivery, etc. But he was concerned about the effect it would have on his natural aggression. So he was also studying tax law, in case he should decide against litigation.

An important part of our self-understanding is our vision of how we would like to develop – who we would like to be. "I wish I were…" Fill in the blank. Everyone can do this. No one will stare at the blank with no ideas. "I wish I were braver, more compassionate, more focused, more self-critical, more relaxed; less competitive, less self-indulgent, less lazy, less affected by my surroundings…" Think of your own list. Now when you reflect that your actions affect your character, you see that you do not have to merely wish. You can move in the direction of your ideal self by choosing the actions that will help you become "more…and less…"

We all feel the tragedy of lost potential. Think of people who died of diseases for which we now have cures. Or of people for whom poverty is the only obstacle stopping them from becoming great scientists, artists, and so on. Or people for whom unjust social policy denied them the means of development. We see the potential going to waste and it is painful. It is painful because the development of that potential would have contributed greatly to improving the world – improving the lives of those individuals possessing the potential, and the lives of others whom they would have touched.

The preciousness of the opportunity to develop our potential applies to many different types of potential. It includes potential for the development of mind and body, sensitivity and perception. It also includes the potential for character development. When we think of "successful" lives, we tend to think of success in economic, artistic, scientific, political terms. We need to also think of success in terms of character development. When we think of the loving son, or the altruist, or the woman who made herself psychologically healthy, and we feel admiration for something precious, we recognize that if the potential to develop that preciousness is lost, it too is a tragedy.

Let's sum up: Actions are expressions of character. Love is the key element in ideal character – the closer to love the motivation is, the higher the value we see in the action and the person. The value of being a loving person is not just that it improves actions. Being a loving person is being the best person one can be.

II. EXPLANATION

Where do these feelings and intuitions come from? What in us leads us to care about character even in cases where character makes no difference to the consequences of action? Why does love strike us as uniquely essential to our humanity? As we noted at the beginning, secular approaches vary from one extreme (moral nihilism) to the others (e.g., evolutionary ethics, psychoanalytic ethics, situational ethics, etc.). So the secular world does not have an accepted answer to these questions. My purpose here is to outline the explanation found in classical Jewish sources.[3]

---

3. Reason to accept the Jewish explanation as true can be found at my website, dovidgottlieb.com, in *Living Up to the Truth*, found in the publications section.

Here is the headline: *Jewish sources see these feelings and intuitions as expressions of the soul. The ability to love is the ultimate fulfillment of the soul.*

Let's start at the beginning and go slowly. The start will be familiar: The world is a creation. It has a beginning, and an all-good, all-knowing, and all-powerful Creator. The Creator has a goal for the world and is guiding the world towards that goal. Nothing in the world can be fully understood without seeing its place in that goal.

Why is there a world? Why was God not satisfied with His own perfection? What could He have needed that motivated Him to create the world? The answer is that God created the world as an act of love. The world exists so that God can bestow His love upon it.[4]

Let's fill in some of the details. *Step 1*: What could God have needed? Here we must make some distinctions. There are (at least) three different ways to need: (1) I need food to satisfy my hunger; (2) I see that you are starving and this causes me pain as I empathize with you. And I need food (to give to you) in order to relieve *my* pain at seeing you starving; (3) I see that you are starving and I need food to relieve your starvation. Let's see how (1), (2), and (3) differ.

1. *I may need food to satisfy my hunger.* Here my need is purely selfish. If I act to relieve my need for food, I act in a com-

---

4. Sometimes it is put this way: God is perfection. One element in perfection is goodness. Perfect goodness means goodness than which there is no better. Now imagine goodness as an unrealized potential. A person stranded on an unpopulated island [except for him] may possess good character, but he cannot express it. His goodness would be more perfect if he had the opportunity to apply it to others who could benefit from it. Thus God's perfection demands a recipient for His potential goodness.

pletely self-centered manner. My concern is with my own condition. Nothing else enters my thoughts.

2. *I see that you are starving and this causes me pain as I empathize with you. And I need food (to give to you) in order to relieve* my *pain at seeing you starving.* Here I am concerned with you – it is your condition that is causing me pain. But in the end, I act to relieve my pain, so my motivation is still self-centered. It is my pain that motivates me to act to improve my condition.

3. *I see that you are starving and I need food to relieve your starvation.* Here I act in order to relieve *your* suffering. I may or not be in pain. But even if I am in pain, that is not the reason for my action. (Remember your helper and your friend's cynical misinterpretation of his actions?) So, strictly speaking I do need something. But acting to fulfill that need is not at all self-centered. My condition is not any part of my motivation. I do not act to acquire something for myself.

Now if we want to describe God's need that motivated the creation, it will be of type 3. He needed nothing for Himself – being all-powerful means that He lacked nothing for Himself. So no selfish benefit could motivate His action. But goodness could (and did) motivate His action. That is a motivation wholly directed at another, the recipient of the good He bestows.

There is a word for this kind of motivation, as we have described it so far – the word is "altruism." But there is another dimension to the motivation of the Creator, one that will need a different word to describe it.

So let's push on. *Step 2:* The motivation is to give good. What kind of good will God give? It will be the greatest good that a creature can possess. To give anything less would compromise His goodness. So what is the greatest good that a creature can

possess? Since God *is* the greatest good, what is best for the creature is to have as much of God's good as possible.

He accomplishes this in two ways that supplement each
other. First, the creature is enabled to become Godlike – to possess characteristics like those of God. Since those characteristics
are parts of God's goodness, when the creature acquires them,
the creature participates in God's goodness directly. But the extent of this participation is extremely limited – it is limited by
the infinite gulf between the Creator and His creatures. So there
is a second way in which God enables the creature to benefit
from His goodness – those characteristics enable the creature
to sustain a love relationship with God. *God gives Himself to His
creature in the relationship of love.* This relationship is the greatest pleasure possible for the creature.

Let's look more closely at each of these ways that God shares
His perfection with us.

The Hebrew language uses certain words to describe both
God and man. Both God and man are called "righteous," "merciful," "loving," "straight," "just," and "gracious." We ought to be
surprised by this. After all, God is the infinite spiritual Creator.
Man is a finite and very physical creature. How could there be
anything in common between them?

Similarly, what is meant when Genesis says that God created man in His "image"? We know that God does not have an
"image" – He has no physical appearance to which the appearance of a person could be similar. And even if we translate the
Hebrew term *tzelem* more correctly as "form," the question remains. What kind of "form" could God have to which a human
"form" would be similar?

Perhaps you will answer that these words are not meant
literally. They are only metaphors. That is certainly correct, but
it leaves open two questions. First, even metaphors are based

upon real similarities. The sky can be ink, and George can be a bear, but the sky cannot be a bear and George cannot be ink! So we will have to describe what real similarity between God and man makes these metaphors possible. Second, Judaism bids us develop in ourselves God's own characteristics. "Just as He is merciful, so you too be merciful; just as He is gracious, so you too be gracious." Even allowing for the inevitable differences of quality and quantity, there must be some common essence to those characteristics that man can share with God so that the commandment can be carried out.

The picture in the sources is this: "Man is created in God's form" means that man is given the capacity to become Godlike. He can acquire characteristics that really are similar to those of God. Man thus comes to share God's perfection. This is the greatest good a creature can possibly possess – to share God's own perfection.

Let's see how this works in a few examples. In what ways can man be Godlike? God's perfection means that He is totally self-sufficient, self-determined. He is what He is only because of Himself. Nothing creates God, nor changes God. Clearly man cannot be exactly like that, completely self-determined; man is a creature! The fact that man is created by God means that man is not *totally* self-determined. But there is one element in man's makeup that enables him to be at least partially self-determined, and that is free will. When man makes free choices he creates by himself changes in the world, and changes in himself (as we saw in #5). Thus, unlike everything else in the creation, man can be partially self-creative, self-determined, and in this respect he can partly resemble God.

God is benevolent. Indeed, we said that His purpose for the whole of the creation was to give good. If man will develop his own loving-kindness, then man will resemble God in the characteristic that underlies all of God's creation. The other Divine characteristics that play a role in the creation – justice, mercy, forgiveness, and so on – provide further examples. To the extent to which a person cultivates those characteristics he will be Godlike in those respects.

Resembling God is a direct, if limited, participation in God's perfection. But this resemblance has a further application – *it makes possible a love relationship with God.*

This is not the place for a full account of love, which is beyond my powers in any case. I hope the following is common enough to be uncontroversial. Love depends upon a certain amount of similarity. If there are very few shared experiences, goals, reactions, values, ideas, feelings, and perspectives, love will be thin at best. Imagine trying to love an ancient idol worshipper who happily engages in child sacrifice. Or a person whose whole life is given to studying the growth patterns of hairs on the legs of fleas. Or someone with an IQ of 200 who has memorized the entire *Encyclopedia Britannica*. These differences from ordinary people make real love extremely difficult. How much more so must be the gulf between God and man! How then can man and God love one another?

God shows Himself to us with certain characteristics, and makes it possible for us to develop similar characteristics. A similarity results that can be the basis of the relationship. And the heart of this similarity is love itself – the capacity to express loving-kindness. *God creates us out of love, gives us the capacity to love, and invites us to love Him, and be loved by Him.*

Now *the soul knows all of this.* It knows that it has the potential to be Godlike and thereby embody and enjoy the greatest possible good. It knows that it is destined to enjoy loving and being loved by God. It knows that its place in this world – embodied, in a physical environment, with God's presence hidden –

is a temporary exile for the sake of its own greatest good. All its other capabilities – for intellectual and emotional and physical development – are only means to Godliness. And the essence of this Godliness is the capacity to love. In the end, this capacity will be used for the most perfect love relationship that can be imagined – the eternal love between the Creator and His creatures. *This is the root of our feeling that love is essential to being a fulfilled human being.*

Jewish sources describe the soul as a princess married to a poor farmer. What can he do to please her? What meals shall he serve, what furnishings shall he provide, what entertainment? She grew up in the palace and received royal treatment and a royal education. She is exiled from all that is fit for her. If her horizons are strictly limited to the farmer's world, she will never be happy.

But imagine that her father still cares for her, and provides her with ways to develop her exquisite talents that she inherited from him, even in the farmer's home. Imagine he communicates to her that eventually they will be reunited. At that time the talents she develops here will be the foundation of her renewed life with her father. Will this not be her lifeline? Will she not measure her life, her goals, and her accomplishments in terms of growth towardss the greatness of her father? For that is her own true greatness – to share the greatness, the perfection of her Father, in eternal love.

This is the source of our intuitions and feelings about the importance of character. These intuitions and feelings spring from the soul. They are the expression of the soul's perception of its true self in a world designed to hide that truth. They are the recognition of Godlike elements in man, and the capacity to develop those elements into ever-greater expressions of qualities similar to the divine.

Let's go back through the scenarios with this perspective in mind. When the surgeon acts out of generosity and sensitivity to provide health, is he not acting in a Godlike way? God creates the world out of benevolence, and the surgeon treats his patients, and makes his expertise available to other surgeons, out of benevolence. And if we discover that this is a mistake and his real motivation is selfish, this removes the similarity to God. The same applies to the case of hypnosis – robotic behavior is not at all Godlike. Our feelings and intuitions are the result of the soul applying the measure of Godlikeness to the surgeon's actions.

The same holds true for altruism. The helper is motivated by the sense of duty and the desire to help others in need. That makes him Godlike, and therefore qualifies him for the title "altruist." For God is the supreme altruist. He acts out of benevolence only. That is why we find altruism admirable.

In the case of the two sons we have a contrast of *relative* Godliness. Both sons do what is right because it is right. As God is righteous, so are they. But God is more than righteous. Indeed, God's righteousness is founded on His loving-kindness, as are all of His attributes. The first son feels a debt to his father for all the good he received. But he does not appreciate his father's loving-kindness – the foundation of his father's Godliness. And this shows that the first son is deficient in his appreciation for loving-kindness. The first son's character does not respond to and does not exhibit loving-kindness. We therefore see less Godliness in him than we do in the second son.

The case of accomplishment illustrates the same theme, but in a different application. We said that the ability to be partially self-determined is both one aspect of Godliness and the basis for all the other aspects. God is totally and absolutely self-determined; man is (partly and relatively) self-determined through free will. So man has some similarity to God in self-determination. And all other aspects of similarity – moral and spiritual characteristics – depend upon free will. Moral and spiritual characteristics are by definition self-created. This is why we admire accomplishment, because the soul knows that all its real good lies in what it does for itself.

This also explains why we mourn lost opportunities. A person with the potential to develop valuable capabilities is a person who could develop Godliness and thereby realize a great good. When external circumstances prevent that development, we feel the loss of that supreme good.

Finally, we now have a much deeper understanding of the rabbi who analyzed the psychological source of his action so as to refine his character. This was his soul yearning for more Godliness. And the same applies to all of our decisions when we take account of their internal effects. We are striving for our own Godliness. The soul knows that other goals will not really satisfy because they do not express man's essence – the form with which God created him.

III. APPLICATIONS

God's purpose for the creation is benevolence, and our purpose is to develop Godlike characteristics, chief among them being benevolence. It is reasonable to expect, therefore, that the commandments of the Torah will express our purpose – the commandments will express benevolence in action and reinforce it in character.

For some commandments this is fairly obvious. Here are some examples.

There are two injunctions to give charity: do not tighten your fist, and do not harden your heart. Now if the fist is open, then the poor receive the money. What is added by requiring that the heart not be hard? It is not enough to give the money: one must also empathize with the pain of the poor. Charity is given with the heart as well as the hand.

The highest form of charity is to enable the poor to earn their own living. We provide jobs, loans to start a business, training, etc. This provides livelihood together with the psychological support necessary for self-respect and dignity. Next highest is anonymous charity – the giver and the recipient do not know each other. This minimizes embarrassment.

"You shall love your friend as yourself." Some take the comparison "as" to refer to the amount of love; others take it to refer to the root of the love (love your friend *with* your self-love). In either case, this is the most sublime expression of the ideal of loving-kindness.

"You shall love the convert." Even though the convert is a full Jew, and so he is included in the previous paragraph, there is an *additional* mitzvah to love him. Considering what he sacrificed, he deserves special consideration.

On the other hand, there are other commandments for which the expression of benevolence is not at all obvious. But when you look deeper, it is there. Sometimes it is a matter of the mitzvah developing a person's character in such a way that it will eventually benefit others. And sometimes it is a matter of hidden connections through which the mitzvah directly benefits others. Here are some examples.

The Torah commands us to love God.[5] Now this appears to be a commandment relating man exclusively to God.[6] But

---

5. There are many questions about this commandment. Can emotions be commanded? What about God makes love the appropriate relationship? Can we know God well enough to love Him? These questions (and others) deserve detailed answers. But I can make my point without addressing them.

6. And in this respect it is already an expression of loving-kindness – to-

it has profound implications for our relations to other people. To see this, imagine loving a person. Imagine that this person has a child who is in danger. Would not our love for the parent lead us to want to help the child? How better could we express our love for the parent than to save his child? Now let us reflect that all people are God's "children." He created them, He is dedicated to their welfare – their spiritual success is the purpose of His creation. If we love God, then we will want His "children" to succeed, and we will work towardss that end. Thus our love for God will lead us to help other people realize their spiritual potential, that is, to have the greatest possible good.

There is a commandment to stand in awe of God. How can we express awe for God? By treating those who represent Him in the world with reverence. Those people who teach God's will, and who give paradigm expression to His will, must be treated with reverence. Thus awe for God will be enacted in our relationships to other people.

One of the most central commandments is Torah study. This appears to be an intellectual challenge, with effect for the student himself. There may be interpersonal aspects to the study process in which others might be benefited, but they seem incidental to the study. Where is there a beneficial effect on others through Torah study? Well, the tradition informs us that *study of Torah maintains the existence of the world.* Were there to be a moment in which no Torah was studied, the world would cease to exist. Thus he who studies Torah is, at that moment, participating in supporting the existence of the world. So, coal miners in China, astronauts revolving about the earth, the stockbrokers on Wall Street – indeed, all people alive at that moment – owe

---

wardss God. My point in the text is that in addition to this direct application of loving-kindness, this mitzvah has implications for interpersonal loving-kindness.

a debt of gratitude to those who are studying Torah at that moment. Now this is a hidden connection. But it reveals the principle by which the Torah defines the goal of all mitzvos in terms of implementing benevolence.

The whole of this picture is captured by a famous incident in the life of the Talmudic sage Hillel. A non-Jew requested to be taught the whole of the Torah while standing on one foot. Hillel said to him: "What is hateful to you, do not do to your friend. This is the whole Torah – all the rest is commentary. Go and learn!" Hillel was basing himself on the verse "Love your friend as yourself."[7] But how can treating others lovingly be the whole of the Torah? Are there not mitzvos that apply only between man and God? Listen to Rashi's explanation: "your friend" can also be God! So the whole of the Torah is to act lovingly to all, God and man alike.

Let's give the rabbi (#5) the last word. The rabbi answered, "The second thought – to split up the money – came from a negative source: '*Don't give* the money to one person…' A thought whose source is 'Don't give' comes from the bad side. That is why I chose the first thought." We now have a much deeper appreciation of him. My actions express my motivations. My soul – my deepest and most true identity – wants to love. If I reinforce that side of me that says "*Don't give…*" then I am weakening that love. So the rabbi searched – where is this thought coming from? Is it coming from the soul that wants to love, or from a selfish element in my psychology that will compromise the soul? The soul will be perfected when our actions are dedicated to and motivated by loving-kindness to all.

---

7. See Maharsha (17th century Talmudic commentator).

Chapter 7

Psychological Benefits of Good Character

Judith Mishell, PhD, *clinical psychologist,*
author of Beyond Your Ego

The fire that broke out at Malden Mills in the winter of 1995
was the largest fire Massachusetts had seen for a century. No
one was killed. But the town was devastated. Malden Mills
was one of the few large employers in a town already in
desperate straits.

"The only thing that went through my mind was, how can
I possibly recreate it," says owner Aaron Feuerstein, the third
generation of his family to run the mill.

"I was proud of the family business and I wanted to keep
that alive, and I wanted that to survive. But I also felt the
responsibility for all my employees, to take care of them, to
give them jobs."

Feuerstein decided to rebuild right there in Lawrence – not
to move down south or overseas in search of cheaper labor.

He also made another shocking decision. For sixty days
following the fire, all employees were paid their full salaries.

"I think it was a wise business decision, but that isn't why I did it. I did it because it was the right thing to do," says Feuerstein.

Most people would have taken the $300 million in insurance and retired.

"And what would I do with it? Eat more? Buy another suit? Retire and die?" asks Feuerstein. "No, that did not go into my mind."

He kept his promises. Workers picked up their checks for months. In all, he paid out $25 million and became known as the Mensch of Malden Mills – a businessman who seemed to care more about his workers than about his net worth.[1]

After these events, Aaron Feuerstein received twelve honorary degrees and was invited as an honored guest to President Clinton's State of the Union Address. What was so special about what he did that he became a national hero? Aaron Feuerstein's actions reflect *menschlichkeit,* or *good character,* and this is obviously a rare commodity in today's world. As Mr. Feuerstein himself said, "I got a lot of publicity. And I don't think that speaks well for our times…At the time in America of the greatest prosperity, the god of money has taken over to an extreme." Mr. Feuerstein says he turns to the Torah, the book of Jewish law, for guidance.[2] He made his decisions based on the verse "You are not permitted to oppress the working man, because he's poor and he's needy."[3] Feuerstein spent the $300 million insurance

---

1. CBS News, "The Mensch of Malden Mills," July 6, 2003.
2. The Torah is comprised of the Written Torah (Pentateuch, Prophets, and Writings) and the Oral Torah (Talmud). Mr. Feuerstein was referring to verse 22:22 from a section of the Writings called *Mishlei* (Proverbs).
3. *Mishlei* 22:22.

money and then borrowed $100 million more to build a new plant that is both environmentally and worker friendly.

His story raises three questions, which this essay will attempt to address: (1) what is good character? (2) why are we so amazed when someone behaves like a mensch? and (3) what are the practical benefits of good character?

What Is Good Character?

According to Rabbi Neil Kurshan, a mensch is a decent, responsible, caring person. "*Menschlichkeit* is responsibility fused with compassion, a sense that one's own personal needs and desires are limited by the needs and desires of other people. A mensch acts with self-restraint and humility, always sensitive to the feelings and thoughts of others."[4] Rabbi Kurshan goes on to say that "The quality of *menschlichkeit* is so fundamental to a person's character that decency and fairness are a part of everything he or she does. It is a basic orientation to life, a way of being in the world, a way of living before God."[5]

In his first book on emotional intelligence (EQ), psychologist Daniel Goleman writes, "There is an old-fashioned word for the body of skills that emotional intelligence represents: *character*."[6] The concept of EQ was coined in 1990.[7] It is a "form of social intelligence that involves the ability to monitor one's own and others' feelings and emotion, to discriminate among them, and to use this information to guide one's thinking and action." Many studies have shown EQ to be more important

4. Neil Kurshan, *Raising Your Child to Be a Mensch* (New York: Atheneum, 1987), 11.
5. Ibid., 106.
6. Daniel Goleman, *Emotional Intelligence: Why It Can Matter More Than IQ* (New York, Bantam, 1995), 285.
7. Peter Salovey and John D. Mayer, "Emotional Intelligence," *Imagination, Cognition, and Personality* 9, no. 3 (1990): 185–211.

than IQ in determining professional, social, and occupational successes.[8]

Psychologists Christopher Peterson and Martin Seligman conducted an intensive cross-cultural search of literature, philosophy, religion, psychology, and other sources of "virtue relevant" information (e.g., greeting cards, bumper stickers, song lyrics, etc.) in order to develop a working definition of character. In their groundbreaking handbook on good character entitled *Character Strengths and Virtues*[9] they identify two main criteria for defining a character strength: (1) "A strength contributes to…the good life, for oneself and for others,"[10] and (2) "Although strengths can and do produce desirable outcomes, each strength is morally valued in its own right, even in the absence of obvious beneficial outcomes."[11] Through their research, Peterson and Seligman were able to classify six core *virtues*:

1. Courage
2. Humanity
3. Justice
4. Temperance
5. Transcendence
6. Wisdom

Each virtue has associated *character strengths*. For example,

8. Goleman, *Emotional Intelligence*, 285; Cary Cherniss, "Emotional Intelligence: What It Is and Why It Matters," paper presented at the Annual Meeting of the Society for Industrial and Organizational Psychology, New Orleans, LA, April 15, 2000.

9. Christopher Peterson and Martin E.P. Seligman, *Character Strengths and Virtues: A Handbook and Classification* (New York: Oxford University Press, 2004).

10. Ibid., 17.

11. Ibid., 19.

"the virtue of wisdom can be achieved through such strengths as creativity, curiosity, love of learning, open-mindedness, and what we call perspective – having an expansive picture of what life entails."[12]

Until a few decades ago, we didn't need professionals and scholars to define good character for us. As Rabbi Kurshan points out, generations of Jewish children grew up hearing the words "be a mensch." Even those of us who grew up in homes where Yiddish was rarely spoken knew exactly what our parents meant by "*zay a mensch*." It meant we should help Mommy, be nice to people, and work hard in school, that we shouldn't lie, steal, cheat, or hit our little sister/brother; and you didn't have to be Jewish to understand the concept.

How was the concept of *menschlichkeit* transmitted through the ages? Through the Torah, which has been the universal foundation of moral education for over three thousand years, teaching us to strive constantly for dynamic spiritual growth and enrichment. Rabbi Zechariah Fendel says, "A vital key in this process of dynamic spiritual growth…revolves around character refinement and improvement of one's character traits."[13]

Why Are We So Amazed When Someone Has Good Character?

Why are these "good and upright traits" so rare that Mr. Feuerstein became a national hero? Why does Rabbi Kurshan feel the need to explain that "*menschlichkeit* is not the same as soft-headedness, indecision, or weakness. A *mensch* is not a

---

12. Ibid., 13.
13. Zechariah Fendel, *The Ethical Personality* (New York: Hashkafah Publications, 1986), xvi.

fool…. Being a *mensch* does not mean passive acquiescence…. A *mensch* does not finish last."[14]

Why do good character and *menschlichkeit* need to be defended? What values have replaced our traditional wisdom and eroded our sense of morality?

First of all, as Mr. Feuerstein said, "At the time in America of the greatest prosperity, the god of money has taken over to an extreme." There is unprecedented affluence in America. Inflation-adjusted income per American has almost tripled since the end of World War II. "A two-car garage was once a goal; now we're nearly a three-car nation. Designer everything, personal electronics and other items that didn't even exist a half-century ago are now easily affordable…"[15] We are consummate consumers, always shopping, always buying, always having new "needs" stimulated by technological advances and Madison Avenue. But this affluence is not making us happier. In fact, social psychologist David Myers reports that the number of people who rate themselves "very happy" has "declined slightly between 1957 and 1998, from 35 percent to 33 percent."[16] Myers concludes that the more we strive for extrinsic goals such as money, the more problems we have and the less subjective well-being we have. The god of money has robbed us of the free time and peace of mind we need to pay attention to the things that really matter.

Peterson and Seligman explain that traditional values have been replaced by "the hedonism of the 1960s, the narcissism of the 1970s, the materialism of the 1980s, and the apathy of the 1990s." Consequently:

---

14. Kurshan, *Raising Your Child to Be a Mensch*, 103–105.
15. Claudia Wallis, "The New Science of Happiness," *Time* 165, no. 3 (January 17, 2005).
16. David G. Myers, "The Funds, Friends, and Faith of Happy People," *American Psychologist* 55, no. 1 (January 2000): 61.

*The United States is facing a character crisis on many fronts...
from the playground to the classroom to the sports arena to
the Hollywood screen to business corporations to politics.
According to a 1999 survey by Public Agenda, adults in the
United States cited "not learning values" as the most important problem facing today's youth. Notably, in the public's
view, drugs and violence trailed the absence of character as
pressing problems.*[17]

Peterson and Seligman say that character has become a prominent topic in contemporary psychology because most people
today seem to believe that character is important after all. Social theorist Amitai Etzioni agrees that we have lost our "moral
voice" and that a return to moral education is crucial.[18]

Other values that have replaced morality based on eternal principles of right and wrong are "political correctness"
(never saying or doing anything that will offend anyone, even
if it means denying the obvious truth or making absurd policy
decisions, like randomly searching little children in airport security), moral relativism (one man's terrorist is another man's
freedom fighter), and individual conscience (you do your thing
and I'll do mine).

Samuel Walker, professor of criminal justice, reveals yet
another facet of the problem: the "rights revolution." He calls
this revolution the most important change of the past half-century. Walker says that this rights culture "involves a new rights
consciousness, a way of thinking about ourselves and others and
our society...an almost reflexive habit of defining all problems
in terms of rights." We express our rights as demands: "I have

---

17. Peterson and Seligman, *Character Strengths and Virtues*, 5.
18. Amitai Etzioni, "Restoring Our Moral Voice," *Public Interest* 116 (Summer 1994).

a right to..."[19] Some of the rights we demand are personal liberty; freedom from unwarranted government regulation, both private and public; the right to openly express our opinions on public affairs; and freedom to live our private lives as we choose. While these rights are not negative in themselves, they must be balanced with an emphasis on responsibilities.

In sharp contrast to our focus on rights, there is no concept of rights in the Torah. The Torah teaches us only about our obligations. If each of us fulfills our obligations, we will all have our rights respected. On the other hand, who will respect our rights if no one pays any attention to their obligations and responsibilities?

Professor of social theory and social action Barry Schwartz identifies another contemporary value that is part of the problem: freedom from constraint. He summarizes his findings this way:

> *Americans now live in a time and place in which freedom and autonomy are valued above all else, and in which expanded opportunities for self-determination are regarded as a sign of the psychological well-being of individuals and the moral well-being of the culture. This article argues that freedom, autonomy, and self-determination can become excessive, and that when that happens, freedom can be experienced as a kind of tyranny...*[20]

Schwartz explains that for the first time in human history, many people can live exactly the kind of lives they choose, without ma-

19. Samuel Walker, *The Rights Revolution: Rights and Community in Modern America* (New York: Oxford, 1998), vii.
20. Barry Schwartz, "Self-Determination: The Tyranny of Freedom," *American Psychologist* 55, no. 1 (January 2000): 79.

terial, economic, or cultural limitations. He sees a dark side to all this freedom from constraint, and provides compelling evidence that having too many options is overwhelming and ultimately unsatisfying. A trivial personal example: I remember standing in front of a counter containing "22 flavors" of ice cream (not to mention yogurt and sorbet). I was overcome by indecision and took quite a long time to make a choice. I finally ordered a "double dip" so I didn't have to choose between two flavors that both seemed irresistible. Nevertheless, the whole time I was eating I kept thinking, "Maybe I should have ordered triple fudge instead of double fudge with chocolate chips..."

It is not such a big deal that my ice cream-eating pleasure was diminished, but it is a big deal to live our lives this way, especially in the moral sphere. But because we value freedom from constraint so highly we are blind to the idea that some of our options may be spiritually toxic and should therefore be off limits. By the time we feel the pain, we may have already made life choices with irreversible consequences, e.g., we may be unwed teenage mothers, or desperately lonely middle-aged adults who can't accept the limitations required to be in a committed relationship. We don't know that the root of the problem is too much freedom and so we keep making the same mistakes over and over.

Rabbi Chaim Shmulevitz[21] points out that permissiveness is a "god" whose essence is the tearing down of all moral and religious restrictions. The only thing that is sacred is the idea that nothing is sacred. "Only too well do we now understand the attraction of this idol. The allure of the ideology of permissiveness and lack of any restraints can be witnessed in contemporary society which faces an onslaught by anarchy and

---

21. Rabbi Chaim Shmulevitz was the head of the Mirrer Yeshiva of Jerusalem.

immorality."[22] As Schwartz concludes, "Freedom of choice is a two-edged sword, for just on the other side of liberation sits chaos and paralysis."[23]

Why are we so shocked when someone behaves in a moral way? Because materialism, hedonism, narcissism, political correctness, moral relativism, individual conscience, the rights revolution, and freedom from constraint have replaced traditional values. In a society that encourages us to do whatever we want, whenever we want, we never experience the deep joy that comes from dedicating ourselves to pursuing worthwhile goals.

The painter who wants to express his artistic vision on the canvas must go through highly disciplined training in order to be able to channel his will through the end of his paintbrush. Once he does this, though, he is then free to paint whatever he wants. So it is with our lives. We have to be reeducated to realize that only through discipline and constraints can we acquire the freedom to express ourselves in a way that leads to true self-respect and self-fulfillment.

What Are the Practical Benefits of Good Character?
I have selected four key character strengths – integrity, kindness, gratitude, and self-regulation – to explore their respective benefits.

Integrity
The score was tied 1–1 and David Tepper was on second base. David was fifteen years old, in the camp's senior bunk and possibly the best player on his team. His team was in high

---

22. Rabbi Chaim Shmulevitz, "Baal Peor," in *Sichos Mussar: Reb Chaim's Discourses; The Shmuessen of the Mirrer Rosh Yeshiva, Rabbi Chaim Shmulevitz, zt"l* (New York: Mesorah Publications, 1989), 249.
23. Schwartz, "Self-Determination," 87.

spirits as he took a lead off second while the next pitch headed towards home plate.

The batter swung and hit a line drive into the outfield. David rounded third and headed for home plate as the crowd roared. There was a play at the plate; as David slid into home, the catcher caught the throw and tagged him. "Safe!" the umpire shouted.

The catcher was obviously upset, and protested. But the umpire stood by his call.

David's team was jubilant. They had taken the lead and were now in a position to pick up some crucial Color War points.

David stood up slowly and dusted himself off. As he walked away from home plate, his teammates surrounded him, pounded him on the back and congratulated him. Strangely, he was the only one who did not seem to be excited. Quietly, he made his way through the crowd and approached the umpire.

"I was out," he said quietly.

The umpire was not sure that he had heard correctly. "What did you say?" he asked.

"I said that I was out," David replied. "I am positive he tagged me before I touched home plate."

The umpire pondered the matter silently. After a very long time, the umpire cleared his throat and said, "Well, I'm human and I can make a mistake. If you're positive that he tagged you before you reached home plate, then you're out."[24]

Definition: Integrity is defined as being true to oneself, living in accordance with one's values and convictions, and practicing what one preaches, even when it is difficult or unpopular.

---

24. Rabbi Shimon Finkelstein, *The Gift of Speech: Refining the Way We Speak* (New York: Mesorah Publications, 2000).

People with integrity take responsibility for their feelings and behaviors and keep their commitments.

Benefits: Research shows that the trait of integrity has many positive psychological, social, and workplace effects.[25] Psychologically, integrity is associated with positive mood, life satisfaction, openness to experience, empathy, self-actualization, and conscientiousness. Psychologists studying motivation have compared the behavior of people whose motivation is authentic or intrinsic (meaning that they are self-motivated and that their behavior is consistent with their own interests and values) with those whose motivation is merely externally controlled (they get a paycheck). They have found that authentic motivation leads to more interest, excitement, confidence, enhanced performance, persistence, creativity, vitality, self-esteem, and general well-being.[26] There is an upward cycle of growth and positive change when people are pursuing self-concordant goals: pursuing and attaining one such goal leads to pursuing and attaining other such goals, leading to overall enhanced personal development.[27]

Socially, integrity is associated with positive relationships – authentic people are better liked than those perceived as lacking authenticity. In schools, educational administrators perceived as possessing integrity inspire more trust in their teachers. In the business world, relationships throughout the organization are more effective when managers are seen as authentic.

For an even deeper understanding of the benefits of integrity we turn to the Torah. The *Gemara* discusses the fact that

25. Peterson and Seligman, *Character Strengths and Virtues.*
26. Richard M. Ryan and Edward L. Deci, "Self-Determination Theory and the Facilitation of Intrinsic Motivation, Social Development, and Well-Being," *American Psychologist* 55, no. 1 (January 2000): 68–78.
27. Peterson and Seligman, *Character Strengths and Virtues.*

the Ark was covered on the inside and on the outside with gold.[28] This is to show us that there should be "no contradiction be-tween one's inner feelings and one's external actions – that one's actions should be in perfect harmony with the feelings in one's heart.... Because it is often difficult to achieve absolute syn-chronization between one's heart and one's action, this praise is reserved only for the truly righteous."[29]

The biblical figure Joseph was a truly righteous person. Be-cause of his exemplary character, he rose from enslavement and imprisonment to become the prime minister of Egypt, second in command only to the Pharaoh. Joseph was not corrupted by his power, nor did he use it to exploit others. In fact, each day, during years of famine in Egypt, Joseph did not even taste a slice of bread until all those who came to him for provisions received their food. He also never took any money that did not belong to him. Since Pharaoh placed his trust in Joseph, Joseph would not misuse his position of authority; rather, the Torah relates, he brought *all* the money to Pharaoh.[30] Joseph received great rewards as a result of his unfaltering integrity. He was freed from captivity, achieved great honor, and acquired enough land for his whole family to settle in Egypt. After his death, Joseph's reputation for integrity continued to bring him rewards. He re-quested to be buried in Israel, and his descendents fulfilled his wishes, carrying his remains through the wilderness alongside the Ark for forty years.

Even when there are no obvious external rewards, a per-son of integrity experiences the deep joy of internal harmony,

---

28. The *Gemara* is the Talmud, part of the Oral Torah. Here we are referring to the *Gemara* in *Yoma*, 72b.
29. Rabbi Daniel Yaakov Travis, *Priceless Integrity: Exploring the Parameters of Truth and Falsehood from a Torah Perspective* (Southfield, MI: Targum Press, 2001), 91.
30. Ibid., 308.

self-respect, and freedom from guilt and regret. Imagine that moment when David Tepper heard the umpire call him "safe." Imagine how much he wanted to be "safe," how much he wanted his team to win, how let down he must have been to feel the "tag" just before he reached home plate. Imagine him hearing the jubilant cries of his friends, knowing that their admiration and excitement were based on an error, worrying that they would be bitterly disappointed when they found out. Imagine the wrenching conflict he felt between the time he heard the umpire's call and the time when he *quietly resolved to tell the truth – no matter what.*

We create ourselves by the choices we make.[31] David's choice to act with integrity was a step towardss becoming/creating a *mensch.*

Kindness

Christmas was a rare day off for my father, Irving Levinsky, since he kept his drugstore open six days a week.... But instead of relaxing on Christmas, when he, as a Jew, had nothing to do, my father would fill up the back of his station wagon with gift poinsettias. Most of these poinsettias he delivered to the poor black and Puerto Rican women who lived in the neighborhood of the store.

After my father retired, he volunteered for the local library to deliver books to shut-ins. Leaning on his cane and limping from his arthritis, he often had to climb flights of stairs to reach the desolate apartments of people, usually younger and sometimes less incapacitated than he, who had run out of reasons to get out of bed.

My father regularly lent money to any of the drugstore

---

31. Rabbi Yechiel Michel Tucazinsky, *The Bridge of Life* (New York: Moznaim Publishing Corp., 1983).

customers who asked him. Most of these loans were never re-
paid. When we were sitting shiva (seven days of mourning)
for my father, Carl, the Italian pharmacist who bought the
drugstore from him, told us how, when my father was trans-
ferring the store over to him, they came upon a one-inch-thick
notebook, filled with entries. Carl asked what it was. My
father replied that this was his record of outstanding loans.
Carl asked how much it was worth. Tossing the book into the
wastebasket, my father shrugged, "It's priceless."

The day after my father died, his rabbi came to talk to
the family in preparation for the funeral.... The rabbi asked
the various family members gathered in the living room if
there was anything special we wanted him to include in the
eulogy.

An amazing scene of revelation unfolded. As each mem-
ber recounted the tales of my father's acts of kindness that he
or she had personally witnessed, the rest of us learned about
many of them for the first time. My father never talked about
his own good deeds, not even to my mother.

But there was also a revelation for me.... I saw that deeds
are what primarily count.... Standing beside my father's body,
gazing at his luminous face, I was shocked to realize who he
had become by virtue of his deeds alone.[32]

As we said, we create ourselves by the choices we make.

Definition: Kindness and the related terms generosity,
nurture, care, compassion, and altruism, involve giving of oneself to others without expecting anything in return. The giving
can be emotional, for example, giving love, support, validation,
sympathy, or empathy; or it can be giving something tangible,

---

32. Sara Yoheved Rigler, "Of Angels and Poinsettias," aish.com, March 5,
2004.

such as flowers, money, food, a ride, a visit to a sick person, or cookies for the Little League bake sale.

Benefits: Psychologist Sonja Lyubomirsky studies what makes people happy. She asks people to carry out an act of kindness once a day for five days, or five acts in one day for a period of six weeks. They can do any act that benefits other people or makes others happy, usually at some cost to self, e.g., donating blood, helping a friend to write a paper, or visiting an elderly relative. The results are very impressive, showing that acts of kindness can cause a significant increase in a person's overall happiness and self-esteem.[33] Lyubomirsky says that she believes her work is revealing the secrets of a life well lived.[34] As you will see below, this "secret" was revealed long ago by the Torah.

Most people who help others experience a "helper's high," or a kind of euphoria. They experience warm feelings, increased energy, satisfaction, enhanced self-esteem, calmness, and relief from emotional stress and the symptoms associated with it. The psychological benefits of kindness do not result from donating money or volunteering for projects that don't involve close personal contact with other people, e.g., sealing envelopes for a charity mailing. In order to reap these immediate rewards, the kindness must involve some kind of human interaction.

Seligman found similar results when he gave his students an assignment to do something purely enjoyable, and to then do something philanthropic. When the students did something that was fun, like hanging out with friends, they enjoyed it, but "when it was over, it was over." When they did an act of kindness

---

33. Sonja Lyubomirsky, Kennon M. Sheldon, and David Schkade, "Pursuing Happiness: The Architecture of Sustainable Change," *Review of General Psychology* 9, no. 2 (2005): 125.
34. "Pursuit of Happiness May Be the Secret to Well-Being," *Tulsa World*, July 5, 2002.

for someone which involved *using their own skill and relating to the recipient* they felt better the whole day. Not only that, but as one student reported, "People liked me more. I could listen better. I was mellower."[35] Less personal acts like giving five dollars to a homeless person did not yield the same positive effects.

So we see that giving, personal relating, and subjective well-being are all connected. This is not surprising in light of the major findings of previous psychological research on what makes people happy, which suggest that people who enjoy close relationships are happier and cope better with life's stresses. *We are happier when we are with other people.* Rabbi Dessler points out that we were created as social beings so we would have the opportunity to become givers. How could we ever experience the helper's high if we were self-sufficient and didn't have other people around to whom we could give?

Rabbi Dessler makes a deeper point about giving – that love flows in the direction of giving; *we love those to whom we give.* It follows that the closer the relationship and the more frequent the contact, the more opportunities we have to give – and then the more we love. The intense and unconditional love of parents for their children illustrates this idea. Findings based on data pooled from surveys of over fifty thousand respondents showed that married people consider themselves happier and more satisfied with life than their unmarried peers, and than those who are separated or divorced. Married people also suffer less from depression.[36] Why? As Rabbi Dessler explains, marriage provides the maximum opportunity for giving, and

---

35. Transcript of a speech given by Martin E.P. Seligman at the University of Pennsylvania's Lincoln Summit in September 1999, full text at http://www.ppc.sas.upenn.edu/lincspeech.htm#top.
36. Myers, "The Funds, Friends, and Faith of Happy People," 61.

hence the maximum opportunity for the development of love and well-being.

Other research shows that among older adults living in community dwellings, volunteering increased longevity.[37] So, it seems that by helping others, we feel better, have better relationships, love more, and live longer. Why do acts of kindness have such a powerful effect on our well-being?

In the physical realm, the answer seems to lie in the release of endorphins, the body's natural pain-reducing chemicals. Harvard cardiologist Herbert Benson notes that people have been searching for millennia for techniques on how to forget oneself, how to lower metabolic rates, blood pressure, and heart rates. He concludes that altruism facilitates the body's ability to shift into the relaxation response, or a deeper state of rest, just as yoga, meditation, and other spiritual practices do.[38]

What holds us back from taking advantage of this amazing panacea? The Torah teaches us that we are dual creatures, body and soul. The soul wants us to do what is right, what will elevate us spiritually, and serve our long-term well-being. The body wants immediate satisfaction of its drives and lusts, regardless of the consequences. Imagine yourself tired and hungry after a long day's work. Your body aches for rest and food. You are on your way home and you see a car parked on the shoulder of the road. A woman with a young child is standing beside the car. Your body says, "Keep going! Someone else will help her." Your soul says, "Stop! Find out what she needs and help her." If you value self-gratification you will keep going. If you value spiritual growth through self-transcendence, you will see this as an

---

37. Peterson and Seligman, *Character Strengths and Virtues.*
38. Allan Luks, "Helper's High: Volunteering Makes People Feel Good, Physically and Emotionally," *Psychology Today* (October 1988): 39–42.

opportunity not only to help someone, but to strengthen your character…and you will stop.

What will help us to strengthen our spiritual strivings so we can overcome the urge for self-gratification and become givers? Rabbi Dessler explains that giving flows from the feeling of blessing and abundance that arises from focusing on what we have, and appreciating that we have it. The taker's mentality flows from a feeling of deficiency that arises from focusing on what we don't have, and not appreciating what we do have. We become givers by learning to recognize the manifold blessings in our lives, e.g., "My car is working well, I have a job, I have food at home in the fridge, I'm in good health," etc. As our awareness of blessing increases, we begin to feel so happy and "full" that we overflow, and naturally want to share what we have with others. As Rabbi Dessler says, "the heart of one in a state of joy broadens to encompass all who are close to him; the more joyful the person the greater his desire that all his friends take part in his joy."[39] An uplifting cycle is created: the more we grow spiritually, the more joyful we are, and the more we want to give – and the more we give the more we grow.[40]

Gratitude

When Marlene Beitel was a young girl growing up in Williamsburg her family lived in a one-bedroom apartment. She and her sister slept on a sofa bed in the living room. Her parents owned a store and worked long hours. The clothes she and her sister wore were mostly home sewn or hand-me-downs. Marlene en-

---

39. Rabbi Eliyahu E. Dessler, *Strive for Truth!* (New York: Feldheim Publishers, 1978), 142.
40. Notice the interrelationship between the character strength of giving and the next one we are going to discuss, gratitude. We become givers by becoming grateful, and as you will see, giving increases our gratitude.

joyed window shopping but never really dreamed of purchasing anything. One afternoon, however…

> …*my eyes became riveted on a deep blue, silky skirt…. Five shiny gold buttons, halfway down the front, gave it an especially stylish look…and wouldn't you know it would be the most expensive item in view: $4.99…. My budget was light-years away from such a luxury.*
>
> *Now, at age fifteen, a Blue Skirt had entered my field of vision and invaded my thoughts…. in spite of all good intentions to the contrary, I must have mentioned The Skirt in passing. Perhaps it was an emotional quiver in my voice that caused my mother to glance up suddenly from stirring pots on the stove one evening…. Sounding casual, she inquired as to the location of the store.*
>
> *One evening my mother came home bearing a package. She smiled mysteriously as she placed it on the enamel table. "This is for you."*
>
> *As I glimpsed the name of the ladies' apparel store, I could feel my heart pounding…. It was simply inconceivable, but there nestled amid the white tissue paper, was surely the world's most divine, dark Blue Skirt…. This glorious, glamorous creation now actually belonged to me…. How special I felt!*
>
> *After about a week I noticed that two of the gold buttons weren't spaced evenly…. My gold buttons were smaller, with a different design…. Slowly the truth dawned on me. In my naïveté, my gullibility, I had been decidedly duped. Deceived. Disillusion engulfed me. What an utter fool I had made of myself. What of my essential worth now? Had my dream creation been sewn from a remnant of material salvaged from a box outside a bargain store?*

It took decades. I was already a mother of teenagers be-
fore I could appreciate the fact that the expenditure of self –
the selflessness – was of ultimate, intrinsic value, that this was
the greatest gift by far. In my middle-aged mind's eye, I could
see my weary mother going blocks out of her way, could feel
her excitement as she made a note of each detail, could empa-
thize with her exhaustion as she bent over the sewing machine.
All this had been lost on the adolescent I once was.

(Years ago, I suddenly recalled the long-forgotten epi-
sode, and tried saying a much-belated "Thank you." But my
mother didn't recall it at all. She was already in her eighties.
I had waited too long.)

It takes living to appreciate giving.[41]

Definition: Gratitude is a sense of thankfulness and appreciation for life and for its manifold blessings. The "gratitude attitude" requires us to recognize, acknowledge, and appreciate
what we are given.

Benefits: The benefits of gratitude are staggering, so impressive that psychologist Charles Shelton concludes that gratitude
is a vital part of the well-lived life.[42] The research on gratitude
speaks for itself....

Psychologists Robert Emmons and Michael McCullough
conducted a series of studies in which students kept daily journals about five things they were grateful for in the past week (the
grateful group), five hassles from the day (the hassles group),
or five events that affected them in the last week (the events

---

41. Malka Adler, "The Blue Skirt," in *A Sunny Slice of Life: Looking Up When
    Life Tries to Pull You Down* (Southfield, MI: Targum Press, 2001).

42. Charles M. Shelton, "Gratitude: Considerations from a Moral Perspec-
    tive," in Robert A. Emmons and Michael E. McCullough, *The Psychology
    of Gratitude* (New York: Oxford University Press, 2004).

group). Students in the grateful group reported feeling more grateful, felt better about their lives as a whole, and were more optimistic about the future than students in the two other comparison groups. They felt more joyful, enthusiastic, interested, attentive, energetic, excited, and determined than those in the hassles condition. They were also more likely to have helped someone with a personal problem or to offer emotional support to someone. They had fewer health complaints and even spent more time exercising. In a study with adults who suffered from neuromuscular diseases, the gratitude group showed more positive emotion and satisfaction with life, and these results were confirmed by the "significant others" in their lives.[43]

There is also evidence that gratitude is an effective coping mechanism for dealing with stressful events. In a study with victims of trauma, grateful people were found to have significantly lower PTSD (post-traumatic stress disorder) symptoms than less-grateful individuals. Another study had trauma survivors rate the emotional impact of the trauma at the time it occurred, and also how the event affects them now. Grateful and less-grateful subjects report the same level of distress at the time of the trauma, but grateful subjects show significantly more emotional healing than their less-grateful counterparts.[44]

One explanation of why gratitude should help us cope is that it helps us reframe memories of negative events as "redemptive sequences," which allows us to find the good in these otherwise unhappy experiences. Typical redemptive sequences are (1) being injured in an automobile accident and after a long, painful recovery, appreciating life much more; (2) being a substance abuser and after "hitting bottom" finally "getting my life together"; and (3) failing out of college and finally understand-

---

43. Emmons and McCullough, *The Psychology of Gratitude*, 174.
44. Ibid., 178.

ing "the value of hard work to achieve my goals." People whose stories are characterized by redemptive sequences tend to be much more satisfied with life, and people who live with the attitude that life itself is a gift are more likely to find something good in what might otherwise be perceived as bad.[45]

According to Seligman, grateful people place less emphasis on material acquisition; they are less likely to judge their own and others' success in terms of possessions; they are less jealous, and they are more likely to share what they have. They are more open to experience, more conscientious, more extroverted, more agreeable, and less neurotic, and they might even live longer. In a study that looked at early-life autobiographies, positive emotions such as contentment, gratitude, happiness, hope, and love were associated with increased longevity.

Seligman says that the single most effective way to turbo-charge your joy is to make a "gratitude visit." This could be writing a letter to thank a teacher, grandparent, or anyone else to whom you feel a debt of gratitude. Then, follow up by visiting the person and reading him or her the letter. The effects of a gratitude visit are truly remarkable. People who do this just once are measurably happier and less depressed up to a month later.

Not surprisingly, gratitude helps to build positive relationships. People who acknowledge and appreciate the good they receive feel loved and cared for. They do more acts of kindness (e.g., lend money, provide compassion, sympathy, and emotional support) and engage less in destructive anti-social behavior. Over time their actions build and strengthen their social bonds and friendships. These bonds are social resources in time of need and help to build a society based on goodwill.[46] As it says in Ecclesiastes 4:9–10, "Two are better than one...for if they fall

---

45. Ibid., 179.
46. Seligman, Lincoln Summit speech.

one will raise his comrade; but woe to him who is alone when he falls and there is no other to raise him."

Ira Byock, a palliative care physician, includes gratitude as one of the four things that matter most in life. He reports that terminally ill patients frequently achieve a state of joy when death is close simply because,

> *Each moment and each human interaction become precious. People who are dying don't take things for granted. In the naked honesty and vulnerability that accompanies proximity to death, even seemingly inconsequential interactions – or simply the presence of another person – can be revealed for the miraculous gifts that they are. Gratitude and joy are intimately fused, and practicing gratitude is a sure way to bring joy into our lives.* [47]

How can we understand the awesome power of gratitude? C.S. Lewis wrote that we "delight to praise what we enjoy because the praise not merely expresses but completes the enjoyment..." [48] When we give, we give of ourselves. Whether we bring chicken soup to a sick neighbor, spend an hour listening to a friend in distress, or give a cold drink to the gardener on a hot day, we are giving of ourselves (our time, energy, and resources). If the recipient acknowledges what is given and *feels grateful*, he is saying, "I appreciate *the goodness in you* from which this kindness flows." [49] He accepts our gift of self, and now, part of us is in the recipient. If the receiver is a giver, he will immediately want to

---

47. Ira Byock, *The Four Things That Matter Most* (New York: Free Press, 2004), 105.
48. Philip C. Watkins, "Gratitude and Subjective Well-Being," in Emmons and McCullough, *The Psychology of Gratitude*.
49. I am indebted to Rabbi Shlomo Holland of Lakewood for this deep insight into gratitude.

give something in return, and when we *appreciate* and receive his *gift of self,* a part of him enters into us. We, in turn, want to give more, creating a feedback loop between us, a positive flow of giving, receiving, feeling gratitude, and giving in return. This cycle creates a feeling of unity and love, which creates extremely powerful bonds over time. Since we human beings long for connection, our joy is enhanced and completed when our gratitude connects us to each other.

Understanding this dynamic can help us strengthen and deepen all of our relationships and have a transformative effect on our lives.

Self-Regulation

The last three years of Rabbi Avrohom Grodzensky's life were spent in the Kovno Ghetto.[50] Throughout his life he worked diligently to strengthen his faith in the face of tragedy and adversity, and these three years were the crowning chapters of his life. His ability to maintain equilibrium and to rise above fear, personal suffering, and grief were an inspiration to all around him in those dark days.

> *The Kovno Ghetto…the word ghetto by itself evokes hardship, suffering, pain and distress, but mention of the Kovno Ghetto should bring on quaking and trembling. Nobody will ever be able to imagine what life was like there….*[51]
>
> *The ghetto was to house thirty thousand people crowded into an area that had previously housed eight thousand….*

---

50. Rav Avrohom Grodzensky was the spiritual leader of the Slobodka Yeshiva in Kovno, Lithuania.
51. Rabbi Yitzchok Elchonon Gibraltar, a survivor of the Kovno ghetto, in M. Musman, "The Tzaddik Who Ruled through His Fear of Heaven: Sixty-one Years since the Martyrdom of HaRav Avrohom Grodzensky, zt"l, Hy"d," *Yated Ne'eman,* July 22, 2005.

Incarcerating the Jews in the ghetto allowed the Germans to squeeze every drop of slave labor from them...while conducting periodic selections and murdering huge numbers of the population as and when it suited them.

One day...signs were posted that on the morrow, instead of going out to work, each of every one of the ghetto's twenty-six and a half thousand inhabitants was to come to the main square.... By the end of the day, ten thousand men, women and children...were taken to the Ninth Fort and murdered. The clacking of the machine guns could be heard all day long in the ghetto.

The survivors were stunned and broken. No family was left intact; all had returned home with some family members missing.... The sounds of hysterical weeping were heard from every house. People could neither eat nor sleep.[52]

Rabbi Grodzensky and his daughter survived the slaughter. She reported that every Friday morning the surviving Torah students would meet in their house and her father would teach them Torah and give them support and encouragement. The students,

...broken in both body and spirit, [were] left by themselves, sole survivors of their entire families...continually starving.... It wasn't easy for them to maintain concentration and listen. Their weakness, hunger and exhaustion almost overwhelmed them. But the words of comfort and encouragement that Father lavished upon them were a wellspring of support that gave them the strength to continue without breaking.

It is hard to understand what emotional resources Father drew upon that enabled him to maintain his concentration for

---

52. M. Musman, "The Tzaddik Who Ruled through His Fear of Heaven."

learning and to give encouragement to all those around him under the harsh ghetto conditions.... Yet he continued doing so throughout all the years of the ghetto's existence.

 It is fascinating to note that Father was always calm. His face was always serious but it always radiated tranquility. His face continued shining in the ghetto's darkness...despite the fact that starvation left its mark on him; he grew very thin indeed, to the point where he could hardly be recognized.

 Father's tranquility had an effect upon those around him.... And in our house, those wounded, grieving souls found calm.... Without question, the hour that they spent with Father gave them the emotional resources and the strength that they needed to continue along their paths of suffering. Not once did Father complain, nor did he ever express his worries.[53]

Rabbi Grodzensky was hospitalized after he received a crippling blow from the Germans when they found him hiding with his son. On July 13, 1944, the Germans burnt the hospital, with all of its patients inside.

A Yeshiva student was the last to report a visit with the great and righteous sage. He reported Rav Grodzensky's last words to him, "I do not care what happens to me. My pain will not cause me anguish. I will suffer from hearing the groans of my brother and sisters and the little children as they are asphyxiated by the fire."[54]

Definition: Self-regulation is the ability to control and channel impulse in the service of achieving a goal, to regulate our

---

53. Ibid.
54. Ibid.

emotions, and to defer gratification. Goleman calls self-discipline the "bedrock of character."[55] It is a basic emotional skill, one that used to be well known as "will."

Benefits: Almost all of life's hardest struggles boil down to the choice between the demands of some internal drive, and doing what we think is right, or what we know will be good for us in the long term. "I feel like staying in bed, but if I'm late again I'll lose my job." "I'd love a chocolate éclair for dessert, but I really want to lose weight." "I know I told Mom I would stop in on the way home, but I'm too tired. I'll just tell her I have to work late and can't make it." Because these moments occur in such widely disparate circumstances, we may not realize that at the root, they have in common an underlying self-regulation issue.

Seligman writes that "self-regulation failure is central to nearly all the personal and social problems that currently plague citizens of the modern, developed world. These problems include drug addiction and abuse, alcoholism, smoking, crime and violence, unwanted pregnancy, sexually transmitted disease, underachievement in schools, gambling, personal debt and credit card abuse, lack of financial savings, anger and hostility, failure to exercise regularly, and overeating."[56]

In a fascinating study that demonstrates the importance of self-restraint, four-year-olds were escorted to a room by a researcher and told that the escort had to run an errand. If they could wait for him to return, they could have two marshmallows. If they couldn't wait they could have one marshmallow, left where they could reach it, right now. Some of them were able to wait fifteen to twenty minutes for the researcher to return. They came up with many strategies to help them resist temptation. Some covered their eyes, some rested their heads in

---

55. Goleman, *Emotional Intelligence*, 285.
56. Peterson and Seligman, *Character Strengths and Virtues*, 506.

their arms, some talked to themselves, others played with their hands or feet, sang, or tried to sleep. The more impulsive children grabbed the one marshmallow almost immediately after the experimenter left the room.

The study tracked down the children when they were graduating from high school. The emotional and social differences between the two groups of children were striking! As adolescents, those who resisted temptation at four were more socially competent, self-assertive, and better able to cope with frustration. They were less likely to get rattled and disorganized under pressure or regress under stress; they accepted challenges and persisted rather than giving up in the face of difficulties; they were more self-reliant, confident, and trustworthy; they took initiative; and were still able to delay gratification for a desired goal. They were far superior as students, more articulate, better able to concentrate, and more eager to learn; and their SAT scores averaged 210 points higher.

The children who grabbed the one marshmallow tended as teenagers to avoid social contacts, were more stubborn and indecisive, had less tolerance for frustration, lacked self-worth, were immobilized by stress, were more prone to jealousy and envy, reacted to annoyances with a sharp temper and thus got into more arguments and fights, and were still unable to delay gratification.[57]

Another follow-up study was done when the children had grown up and were in the workforce. The same pattern of intellectual and emotional differences between the two groups was

---

57. Yuichi Shoda, Walter Mischel, and Philip K. Peake, "Predicting Adolescent Cognitive and Self-Regulatory Competencies from Preschool Delay of Gratification," *Developmental Psychology* 26, no. 6 (November 1990): 978–986.

found, and it became clear that these differences also affected them in their work.[58]

Other studies show that people with a high degree of self-control[59] report fewer pathological symptoms, including psychosomatic problems, obsessive-compulsive patterns, depression, anxiety, hostile anger, phobias, paranoid ideation, and psychoticism. They also had better relationships, experiencing more cohesive family life, less interpersonal conflict, and better empathy. People with self-control also tend not to have many impulse control problems. For example, they are less likely to abuse alcohol and illegal drugs, to have eating disorders, and to engage in other anti-social behaviors.[60]

The Ethics of the Fathers 4:1 asks, "Who is strong?" Answer: "He who subdues his internal desires." The verse continues to teach, "He who is slow to anger is better than a strong man, and a master of his passions is better than a conqueror of a city." Jewish thought acknowledges the power of our drives and lusts and understands the fierceness of the struggle between the negative and positive forces within us. The real test of a person's strength is self-control, not control over others. It takes tremendous strength of character to master our passions even though the battle may be an entirely private one – with no parades or medals for the victor.

As we have said before, we create ourselves by the choices we make. When we make choices in the internal struggle, we are either strengthening the negative or the positive forces within us. The Jewish Sages tell us that our passions have a legitimate

---

58. The follow-up was directed by Philip Peake.
59. It is important to note here that we are not talking about *overcontrol* or rigidity. As used here, high self-control means that we can choose if, when, and how to respond to further our own goals.
60. Peterson and Seligman, *Character Strengths and Virtues.*

role in life and should be subdued, not destroyed. The true hero is the person with sufficient willpower to subdue his desires *when he knows they are wrong*. We are all very skilled at justifying our desires and even making them sound noble: "My hostess went to so much trouble to make those éclairs. I better have one or she'll be insulted." So, to be really strong we must also learn to be very honest with ourselves.[61] In order to be honest, we have to ask, "Am I just justifying something I want, or am I really making a moral choice?" We often need to check in with others because our biases are so strong that it is very difficult to be objective.

EPILOGUE: HOW DO WE DEVELOP GOOD CHARACTER AND TEACH IT TO OUR CHILDREN?

As we have seen, the benefits of good character are astounding. We surely all want the benefits of "spiritual fitness," just as we would all like the benefits of physical fitness. We know that to be physically fit takes a lot more than just joining a gym. We need a program tailored to the strengths and weakness of our bodies and our current level of fitness, a program that includes stretching, aerobics, and strength training. *And then we have to do it!* Day after day, month after month, year after year.

The same holds true in the spiritual realm. To develop character strengths takes commitment and dedication to a program of spiritual growth. And the rewards for the disciplined pursuit of spiritual fitness are a happier, more fulfilling life, a life lived with a sense of purpose and the true self-respect that comes from living with integrity.

Moral education has traditionally been the role of religious institutions – and judging from a large body of research,

---

61. *The Ethics of Our Fathers: The Sages' Guide to Living* (New York: Mesorah Publications, 1995).

our rabbis, preachers, and ministers do the job very well. Studies show that religious observance is linked to a wide range of human virtues: gratitude, forgiveness, kindness, compassion, altruism, volunteerism, philanthropy, and a sense of life purpose. The earlier a person becomes involved in religious and spiritual practices, the more developed his character strengths will be.[62] We can't start too soon to give our children a moral education!

In addition to the association with the development of character strengths, there is also a positive correlation between faith and happiness. The people who had the highest scores on a spiritual commitment scale were twice as likely as those with the lowest scores to describe themselves as "very happy."[63] Having a religious worldview also has a positive effect on relationships, particularly the quality of family life. Faith is associated with lower levels of marital conflict, greater perceived spousal support, more consistent parenting, and less conflicted relationships between adolescents and their parents. When there is mutual parental participation in religious activities and a shared perception of marriage as sacred, there is better marital adjustment and lower levels of verbal aggression. Religion also plays a significant role in individuals' efforts to cope with illness and psychosocial stress. Children and adolescents who are assessed to be at a higher level of religiousness show greater emotional self-regulation, are less aggressive, less likely to engage in illicit drug and alcohol use, have better academic records, and tend to delay sexual involvement and other illicit activities.[64]

There are many possible explanations for these associations between faith and well-being. One is that faith communities provide social support; another is that many people derive mean-

---

62. Peterson and Seligman, *Character Strengths and Virtues*, 610.
63. Myers, "The Funds, Friends, and Faith of Happy People," 64.
64. Peterson and Seligman, *Character Strengths and Virtues*.

ing and purpose from their faith. Yet another is that religious worldviews propose answers to some of life's deepest questions and offer hope when confronting the terror we experience in the face of suffering and death.[65]

Perhaps there is another, even more fundamental explanation. Perhaps deep religious faith connects us with God and gives us a way to achieve true joy by fulfilling our purpose in life. As Rabbi Dessler writes, only the Creator knows the true depths of the human soul that He created, and only He knows what makes us truly happy.[66] Perhaps we simply can't be fully satisfied with a life devoid of connection to our ultimate Source.

The Jewish approach to connecting to God is to learn and *live* the blueprint for life given to us by God. The Torah gives us a step-by-step spiritual training program for character development in the form of mitzvos (commandments). The commandments are designed to strengthen our spiritual muscles. For example, we develop self-regulation and the "gratitude attitude" by saying blessings over our food. Before we eat, we stop to acknowledge that our food is a gift from God, and after we eat, we thank Him for that gift. By keeping the laws of the Sabbath we develop a highly sensitive control center that frees us from robotic, automatic behavior. The laws, which may appear to be nothing more than a long list of difficult prohibitions, have the effect of creating a precious island of time; time to strengthen bonds with God, family and friends, and time to renew our dedication to, and focus on, spiritual growth.

Character education is woven into the fabric of Jewish life. Torah principles give us guidance on how to conduct ourselves throughout the day. For example, from the earliest ages, Jewish children are taught to give charity, to do acts of kindness, to

---

65. Myers, "The Funds, Friends, and Faith of Happy People."
66. Dessler, *Strive for Truth!*

give others the benefit of the doubt, and to respect our parents, teachers, and elders in the community. It is well known that role modeling is the most powerful teaching method, and in Jewish life children see their parents saying blessings, giving money to the poor, bringing soup to sick neighbors, taking care of elderly parents, etc. The children are included in these activities whenever possible. All of these moral lessons are further reinforced in the schools. Part of the high school curriculum is the *chessed* (acts of kindness) club, where youngsters take on activities like visiting the elderly or working with handicapped children. Jewish life is a total immersion program of spiritual elevation and character development.

I have personally experienced the uplifting power of Judaism to give life the kind of meaning and purpose that make every moment significant. After being an unaffiliated Jew, I returned to my spiritual roots and became observant. When I started learning and *living* Torah, I began to experience the benefits discussed above. It has been an incredible journey of self-discovery that has connected me to my deeper self, to others, and to God, and the growing continues each day.

As for you, reader, I wish you well on your journey.

The Golden Path: On Being a Mensch

Moshe Kaplan, MD, *physician, investment advisor, and author of* A Wholly Life

In the Jewish worldview, everyone can be a winner. Success is not a rat race between me and the next guy – it is between me and myself (between me and the rats inside me). The rat of selfishness, the rat of unhealthy desires, the rat of laziness, the rat of depression all live within each of us. True success in life means beating these inner rats before they beat us.

Very few people in the world, however, devote much thought, time, or effort to character development and refinement. The inner peace and social benefits that come from good character – from living a life free of jealousy and anger, while being in control of our thoughts, feelings, speech, and actions, and maintaining a deep sense of humility – are so obvious. Yet for some reason, we allow true happiness to escape us by not seriously endeavoring to improve our character traits.

Imagine two people, one standing at the counter of an Execu-Rent-a-Car, the other sitting in Marvin Smith's Rolls Royce

Dealership. Each is about to get his new *Silver Shadow ii*. One is taking delivery of his new car, the other is renting it for a day.

Who gets more pleasure from the Rolls Royce that day, the purchaser or the renter?

The renter knows that in twenty-four hours he will have to return the car. The buyer feels the car is his forever. Things bring us pleasure in life to the extent that we perceive that we own them. This is why physical things can never give us much lasting joy. We know we can't really hold onto physical things. Rolls Royces get stolen. In time they break down. And so do we!

We do get pleasure when we feel we really own something, but the only things we can ever truly own are our good deeds (the fruits of our good character traits). These can never be taken away from us.

In Hebrew, the word for physical possessions is *nechasim*. The word *nechasim* is related to the word *nechaseh* which means "concealed." After a person dies, he no longer has access to his possessions – they are "concealed" from him. Of course, we want to protect our possessions while we're alive, and a person's most valuable physical possession is his body. A person who is, God forbid, diagnosed with cancer, will submit to whatever treatment has the highest degree of probability of a full recovery. Surgery, radiation, chemo – whatever it takes to survive. People also know that removing the malignant cells is inadequate, because a single surviving cancerous cell can reproduce itself and be lethal. Additionally, a malignant growth does not remain localized, but can spread beyond its place of origin to other vital organs.

This is how we must think about those character traits that endanger our spiritual possessions and our general well-being. Greed, envy, hatred, selfishness, vanity, and arrogance are all cancers that must be totally eliminated. Negative traits not only reproduce themselves in all kinds of life situations, but like malignant cancer cells spread to adversely affect other components of one's character.

Malignant character can certainly kill! Some recent studies show:

1. Negative emotions and anger can trigger a stroke (*Journal of Neurology*).
2. Stress may promote an aging of cells (SF study).
3. Acute stress raises cholesterol levels (*Journal of the American Medical Association*).
4. Men with high levels of tension suffer higher rates of heart disease and irregular heartbeats (*Journal of Psychosomatic Medicine*).
5. Depression can cause risk of dying from heart failure, but good character helps your health (American College of Cardiology).
60 Laughter boosts blood vessel health and is good for the heart (University of Maryland medical case study).
7. Americans who attend religious services at least once a week enjoy better than average health and lower rates of illness (University of Chicago study).

A student came to his teacher complaining that he was unable to eradicate a negative character trait. His teacher suggested different methods, but the student said he had tried them all without success. The student pleaded with his mentor to do something to rid him of the bad trait. Then the teacher rebuked his disciple. "What is it with you that you expect instant perfection?"

Character development does not come overnight, regardless of how much effort you exert. Eradication of stubborn character traits takes time as well as effort. Today you achieve a little, and tomorrow you will achieve a little more.

Business people employ accountants and consultants to analyze their operations and to determine how to maximize their profits. Sensible people should give at least as much thought to success in their lives as they do in their businesses. Each asks himself, "Where am I going with my life?" "What am I doing that is of value?" "In what ways am I growing and improving?" "Which practices should I increase, and which should I eliminate?"

Few people make such reckonings, and those who do often do so on their own, without consulting experts. These same people would not think about being their own business analysts and accountants. When it comes to business they're happy to pay top dollar for sound advice.

Jewish ethical works urge us to regularly do a *cheshbon hanefesh*, a personal accounting. We should be at least as diligent in this as our business affairs and consult experts for sound advice.

What guidelines do we use for character development?

The Rambam, Maimonides, suggests the ideal in character is what he calls the Golden Path, the middle way. The Rambam points out that a person who finds that he is leaning towardss any one extreme has a way of getting back to a state of equilibrium. If a person is stingy, he should, for a while, become a spendthrift. When he rids himself of his stinginess, he will then achieve the middle path in regard to money. And so too for any other negative trait.

We hope that reading this book about how good character helps people succeed at the highest levels in all realms of life will help you on the path to becoming a true mensch.